Dedicated to those I've lost
Dad, Valerie, and Eric

And to those I've found
Marie, Tristan, Allie, Xavier, Huey,
Natalie and Brooklynn

FAMOUS WITH 12 PEOPLE

A CAREER GUIDE ON HOW TO BE
AN INTERNATIONALLY RECOGNIZED
EXPERT IN SOMETHING NOBODY
CARES ABOUT

RICHARD BIRD

ISBN: 979-8-9905757-0-7

Library of Congress Control Number: 2024919915

This publication is designed to provide accurate and authoritative information regarding the subject matter covered. It is sold with the understanding that neither the author nor the publisher is engaged in rendering legal, investment, accounting, or other professional services. While the author has used their best efforts in preparing this book, they make no representations or warranties concerning the accuracy or completeness of the book's contents and specifically disclaim any implied warranties of merchantability or fitness for a particular purpose. No warranty may be created or extended by sales representatives or written sales materials. The advice and strategies contained herein may not be suitable for your situation. You should consult with a professional when appropriate. The author shall not be liable for any loss of profit or any other commercial damages, including but not limited to special, incidental, consequential, personal, or other damages.

Book design by Yaseem Nadir.

Edited by Kari Procton.

Printed by Bird & Bird Media LLC, in Denver, Colorado
in the United States of America

First printing edition 2024.

www.famouswith12people.com

TABLE OF CONTENTS

INTRODUCTION & ACKNOWLEDGEMENTS

———————

I never intended this book to be my first. I have other drafts that I have labored over for years, writing and rewriting them or putting half-finished projects away for months or years until I felt struck by the motivation or inspiration to keep typing. But this book flowed from someplace different. I'll share the events that inspired me to pull my ideas and experiences together in the first chapter, but this book became my first because it simply tumbled out of me. My driving passion for writing this book comes from one simple sentiment.

You have something important to share with people.

I don't know what your something important is. It may be a subject, topic, or skill I've never heard of before. It could be something commonplace that appears to have been talked or written about endlessly, but you have a new and disruptive perspective.

Conversely, it could be something extremely complex that you excel at simplifying so everyone can understand it. It could be something critically important to the survival of a people or a culture or an endeavor that brings people together to solve the world's most challenging problems. It could be a craft, trade, or ability that makes that same world a better place or a more beautiful one.

Whatever it is, though, people need to hear you.

It doesn't matter if you are the best at whatever that something is. Being the best will not inspire people to be interested in what you've got to say. Being intelligent, loud, audacious, brilliant, or passionate isn't enough. People won't listen to you because you think they should or because you believe you are an expert.

People will listen to you because they believe you, and they believe in you.

I can't count the number of people who believe in me and have been critical in helping me write this book and succeed in life. My list keeps growing daily as my network expands, and that same network amplifies and extends my voice, reaching new audiences. It doesn't reach that audience through my yelling or shouting but through others sharing my thoughts and observations. Thanking and mentioning every single one of the people on my list is impossible, but there are many who I must acknowledge.

My amazing wife Marie has been on a journey with me that can only be described as wild and adventure-filled. Her never-ending cheerleading and motivation when I need both have more to do with the creation of this book than even my efforts. Thank you, and I love you. This book wouldn't exist without you.

I must pause to give thanks to my late wife, Valerie, as well. She dreamed of a different life for me after her fight with cancer, a life where I would step out, take risks, and live as intentionally and maximally as I possibly could. And be happy. I try to live up to that promise every day.

My mom and dad deserve more than a mention. My mom raised a pragmatic and cynical kid so well that when I drop a perfectly phrased sentence or response, I hear it in her voice.

My dad, "the Captain." The debt I owe him for teaching me how to tell stories that seem so far beyond belief but are so rooted in truth can never be repaid. My father and I are the same; people frequently assume we are telling tall tales and then are shocked and amused when they find out they are all true. In the two and a half years it took to start and finish this book, my father passed away. I'll be forever grateful that I was able to talk to him about many of these stories in this book before he took that last voyage.

I'm so proud of my children, Tristan, Allie, Natalie, Xavier, Huey, and Brooklynn, for their accomplishments. However, their contribution to this book and my life is that they inspire me with their adventures while still trusting me with their questions, concerns, personal passions, and career aspirations.

Thanks to my mentors and guides, Amy Geiger and Ed Roberto. One pulled me into the profession that would become my life's work, and the other taught me about the crazy world of start-ups on an on-call basis. Then there are the incredible business leaders who were responsible for opening doors, extending permission, and even fully enabling the learning and travel that paved the way to this crazy micro-famousness that is the entire focus of this book: Andre Durand, Dave Packer, Jyoti Bansal, and Sanjay Nagaraj.

I'm humbled by the people who've asked me to play a small part in their lives as their mentor. They have become my most trusted friends and regularly challenge me to grow exponentially with their incredible journeys and shared knowledge: David Lee, Trevor Ritz, John Petty, Tyler Reynolds, and Micah Fluellen.

I also thank my dearest friends (both old and new) who cut me no slack, keep me honest and true, and make me better for knowing them: Jan and Jeff Fluellen, Helen Patton, John Kindervag, Dr. Chase Cunningham, Sean Campbell, Kimberly Wolff, Patrick Sheehan, Jeremy Rohrs, Aubrey Turner, Jim Davidson, Len Damico, Tony Fluellen, Ash Diffey, Patrick Sheehan, Tyler Shields, Ben Blanquera, George Kamide, Omkhar Arasaratnam, and Franco Bradley. And without a doubt, my friend since middle school and inspiration for nearly 45 years, my buddy Stacie Rose.

There are a few people who get a double mention. I've watched the authors in my life successfully navigate the writing and publishing process, proving that it can be done. Helen Patton, James Clear, Chase Cunningham, Aaron Janetti, Sue Markovitch, the young and brilliant Fenley Scurlock, and David Lee. Thank you for showing me that no matter how hard it seems or feels, you can pull the words from your brain and commit them to the written word.

There are three more people I had the briefest of opportunities to spend time with who had a monumental impact on the creation of this book by unknowingly confirming many of the principles I discuss, like authenticity, consistency, and passion. Henry Rollins, Terry Crews, and Mick Ebling—thanks so much.

This book is intended to provide you with a key to a lock. A key that you can choose to use or a key that you put into that kitchen junk drawer along with the other keys we collect during our lifetimes.

I genuinely hope that what I share with you about building your career with this guide and becoming recognized as an expert, a leader, or a voice in the marketplace or your community is something you will practice in your personal and professional life. I want you to use this key to unlock things in and around you that you haven't had access to until now.

When you read the last sentence in this book and close the back cover or park it in your digital library, you are the only person who can take the next step. Intent is not the same as action; ultimately, we live in an action and outcome-based world. I hope that I provide at least some small nugget of wisdom that moves you to choose action and seek positive outcomes and "good trouble" in your field, hobbies, and passions.

I hope to hear your voice "out there" because you have something important to share.

BEFORE WE BEGIN

You want me to do what?

What are the table stakes for being micro-famous?

What do you need to think about or be prepared to do? Before diving into all the different recommendations and suggestions on being famous with 12 people, I need to prepare you for some of the fundamental pieces of the formula.

There is a minimum set of requirements to consider.

If any of these requirements set off the "Oh, I could never do that" alarm bells in your brain, please commit to reading the book to the end. Resist the urge to drop the book and run away. If this career guide pushes you out of your comfort zone, great! This journey you are about to embark on or add fuel to will be filled with moments that turn your initial discomfort into, "Oh, you want me to speak in front of 5,000 people? When do you need me?"

Number one on the list for this journey is speaking. Public speaking. Yep, speaking in front of real, live people. I know many people reading this right now are going, "Ohhhhhhh, hell no."

You can't be a voice in the marketplace, the world, or even your neighborhood if you have no voice. And typing things on a cell phone or a keyboard isn't the same as your voice.

The idea that we can interact purely in the digital world and never in the analog (as in IRL) is entirely unrealistic. Virtual reality won't replace the physical handshake, the stage, or a live audience with their responses and emotions. No amount of AI or digital content can replace or displace the power of a single spoken sentence live in front of an audience. Even when recorded, the ephemeral quality of a single, top-of-mind quip or analogy is still a billion times more potent than one incredibly well-crafted social media post.

Speaking in real life is fundamental to becoming famous with 12 people.

Second on the list is personal brand management and branding knowledge. You must be interested and prepared to develop a personal and an associated professional brand. You might resist this requirement initially because of imposter syndrome, but self-promotion is mandatory for building a brand. Branding is a complicated endeavor, as my friends and marketing experts, Kevin Sellers and Nicole Rowe, have taught me over the years. Kevin and Nicole have led branding campaigns for some of the most influential companies in technology. While the experience and the scale of their campaigns are way more in-depth than needed for an individual personality, the basic branding principles are something you need to be interested in developing. Hopefully, the methods and mechanisms I share with you in this book will be a starting point for learning more about branding rather than an ending point.

Writing, in all its forms, is another requirement. Writing is not as critical as speaking or brand management. That might seem a bit counterintuitive. You might think that "publish or perish" applies to the efforts of being a recognized expert or micro-famous in your field. Posting a stream-of-consciousness sentence or two on social media, writing a blog piece, or even responding to a media request are all different writing styles. Writing a book? Another level and type of writing altogether.

Your efforts are promoted more effectively by one type or style of writing than another. You may also find that writing isn't critical to your brand-related efforts. While this isn't likely, people known for their visual art may let that medium do all the talking for them. Writing is only one medium, and "the medium is the message," according to Marshall McLuhan. For most of us, though, writing is the primary medium for extending our message beyond the speaking requirement.

If you doubt my minimization of writing in comparison to other requirements I've listed, consider this. How many times have you commented or re-posted a written piece by someone else but didn't read the whole thing? Our TL; DR culture has done the written word no favors. To be fair, human beings have always been more inclined to read the headlines, not the small print.

The rise of the digital world didn't change this fundamental human flaw, but this human shortcoming can also be used in your favor. Later in this book, I'll share some techniques to capitalize on that reality. Sound bites and headlines can be more powerful than lengthy treatises and manifestos in micro-fame business.

Becoming a master of a writing method that aligns with your strengths, or your message mission is much more important than being the Ernest Hemingway of your area of expertise. Think of writing as the always present sidekick to the superhero, speaking. Your writing focus and distribution channels should complement your brand, emphasize your message, and make you look good. By "make you look good," I'm simply encouraging you to consider using spell and grammar checks on what you produce. Poor writing is like a smile with a broken tooth right in the middle. It doesn't matter how hard you try to make that smile look good; people will always focus on that broken tooth first. Consider the quality of your writing to be an extension of the quality of your personal image and character.

Depending on your age and personal management skills, the next table-stakes requirement on the list may strike even more fear than public speaking. Social media and all that it requires is, without a doubt, a fundamental component to building your brand, expanding your message reach, and amplifying your voice. While almost everyone has a love/hate relationship with social media, there is no denying the power and the value of the instantaneous communication channels it provides.

Social media will appear frequently throughout this book, but you don't have to become a ninja on every platform. Much like the broader writing topic, I encourage people to become adept at the best platform for them and their constituents and audience. Each platform has distinct strengths and weaknesses and different structural and creative demands. For example, I have never mastered the short forms of social media (Twitter/X, Telegram, etc.), but LinkedIn is a fantastic match for my efforts and interests. My firm belief is that attempting to utilize all the available social media platforms runs the risk of spreading your effectiveness and your message too thin.

A-jack-of-all-trades, but-a-master-of-none kind of problem often results from these attempts.

The final skill or focus required for this journey is flexibility. Rarely will this trip follow the hard and fast plan you craft for yourself. Instead, you'll face choices, chances, and opportunities that, at first blush, feel like luck or chance. That will never be the case. Instead, these moments will be serendipitous and come with the necessity of a choice on your part. Flexibility will be the fuel that powers you to make the right choices in those moments. Being inflexible will create self-inflicted roadblocks to your growth, success, and future.

The list of table stakes, then, are:

- Speaking
- An interest in building or extending your brand
- Writing in one or more of its many forms
- Leveraging social media channels
- Fostering and maintaining maximum flexibility

You may already be doing some, none, or all these things. If it is none, don't let that stop you. Let's get you started on this journey! If you are doing some of them, let's expand your toolkit. If you are currently doing all these things, I hope I can provide a perspective, method, or thought that will lead you to even greater success.

If you do not desire to achieve micro-fame, you can benefit from growing your skills and capabilities in the table-stakes items I have listed. The world needs people who can communicate ideas, champion new thinking, or be the voice for others who have none. You don't have to be on a stage or podcast interview to be one of those people.

I hope that you are still with me. And I hope you are ready and willing to consider things outside your comfort zone that might make you curious to learn more. If all of this seems achievable and you are motivated, let's start on becoming an expert or a voice in your field or community.

Let's get famous with 12 people!

ACCIDENTALLY (MICRO) FAMOUS

What exactly is micro-fame, and why should you care? How can achieving it boost your career and personal growth? In this chapter, we'll explore what micro-fame is, why it matters, and how it can unlock new opportunities for your professional and personal development.

This career guide is the primary result of a singular truth. What is that singular truth?

I have a weird life. I mean it. Weird.

I have been interviewed and quoted in the New York Times, on CNN and NBC, in The Financial Times, on the Closing Bell on Bloomberg, and more blogs and podcasts than I can count. If you search for #theguywiththebowtie, you'll find my smiling face staring back at you from your screen.

In certain social and professional circles, whether digital or in real life, people I have never met recognize me. The alignment of certain social media algorithms and prominent city locations hosting a specific type of conference always produces one result. People in these circles know who I am. People I have never met stop me when I am walking on the street and ask me where my bow tie is. I've been asked for my autograph and to take selfies with strangers. I can walk into a conference hall, and 3000 people know who I am. I am always humbled to know that those 3000 people are there to hear what I say. Even with all this recognition I experience, something about it is wild. None of those people know WHO I am in my daily life. Sure, they know my name, I frequently wear bowties, and what I have to say about a niche topic. They know my brand, message, and professional experience.

This weird life doesn't come with a mountain of random perks. I'm not getting to go backstage and meet the Foo Fighters whenever Dave Grohl swings by my favorite music festival. I don't get handed first-class tickets for flights to far-off places. There are no free dinners when the server recognizes my face from a local TV broadcast the day before. There are no private jets or endorsement deals. I should consider securing a bowtie sponsorship, but I haven't been approached by anyone yet. (We will get to the bowtie thing, I promise.)

This recognition is a relatively new thing in my career. It's only been the case in the last few years. My family thinks this known-personality thing is weird, too. My dad is always super proud of any media coverage I get. He's quick to share it with his friends, and I like to think it is payback to him for not being able to brag about my athletic skills or genius IQ when I was a kid. I was born with neither of those characteristics nor any other intellectual gifts that warrant texting everyone he knows.

So how did this whole Famous with 12 People career guide come to be?

When my dad gets excited about my contributions to my field, the stories of emails I've shared with Jim Cramer at CNBC, or the pictures on the conference keynote splash page, I always say the same thing.

I'm famous with about 12 people.

I'm famous in the same way that the world's best plumber is famous with other plumbers. I'm famous in the same way that the current Guinness Book of World Records record holder of the most hula hoops kept spinning at one time is famous in hula hooping circles.

When I walk out of a conference hall after a killer presentation where people come up to me, expressing how closely they relate to and need to hear what I say, I know my fame is limited to that space. When I walk outside and join the general population, most people have no idea who I am or what I do. It doesn't upset me that this is the reality I live. I'm not unhappy about the small slice of fame that I occupy. I don't yearn for more fame. I don't want to be the Brad Pitt of my profession or the Kim Kardashian of my social media channels. I never think, "Gee, I wish I was the Tom Brady of what I do and got the same kind of attention that he gets."

Truthfully, I love exactly where I'm at on the famous scale. I love it because what I share with my audience is important to them and me. I love it because I'm given incredible opportunities to meet amazing people and travel to places I never dreamed I'd be able to visit. I've gotten to participate in so many incredible experiences.

I interviewed childhood heroes like Henry Rollins, a dream come true for a kid who grew up listening to punk rock. I have spent time with Terry Crews, and within 5 minutes of our first discussion, I realized we grew up within 90 minutes of each other. I met Valterri Bottas and asked him on a live interview feed if Sacha Baron Cohen accurately represented an F1 driver when he played one in Talladega Nights. He responded, "Yes, he was." I laughed until my sides hurt while talking with Frank Caliendo. He rattled off impersonations so fast that it was like comedy speed racing.

I have had the honor to hang out with these and other "Famous with 12 People" personalities with a mission and purpose that is way more important than mine. A great example is Mick Ebling of NotImpossible Labs. He and his team have built homegrown eye readers and machines that construct low-cost prosthetic limbs for victims of war and terror. I mean, this guy should be famous with millions of people. I encourage everyone reading this book to research how Mick Ebling's mindset can change the world and share it with everyone you know.

I know that many or even all the people I mention above may be unknown to you. That awareness further proves the point. They all have huge followings and are known for being very good at what they do in their respective fields.

My "Famous with 12 People" life is not bad. It is a lot of fun.

Now, what the heck is it that I'm micro-famous for?

If you haven't cheated by now and done a Google search, you might wonder what I am known for. Even an internet search may have been disappointing because there are two other FW12P (Famous with 12 People) named Richard Bird. One is an actor, and the other was an Oxford mathematician and professor emeritus. I will share more information about these other Richard Birds in a bit.

I am the micro-famous Richard Bird and considered an internationally recognized cybersecurity expert. I should be more precise. I'm considered an expert in the specific domains of identity-centric security and API security. I'm also known for the same reputation in data privacy and digital consumer protection.

If you are plugged into the cybersecurity or tech development landscape, I'm sure you are thinking something along the lines of, "Damn, that is incredible! I'm holding the book written by the guy who some people call the identity legend. I think I saw him called the father of identity once!" (That situation was embarrassing, believe me.) "This is fantastic. A career guide written by Richard Bird! Everyone has heard of him!" Suppose cybersecurity or the tech world never crosses into your professional atmosphere. In that case, you are probably like the folks in the big city outside the conferences I speak at, oblivious to my existence until you picked up this book.

See how micro-fame works?

Most days, I find any effort on my part to describe this phenomenon and what I'm known for to be hilarious. On other days, it's just bizarre. It feels unnatural when I use the term "expert" in reference to myself, making me chuckle every time I do. If there is something I don't consider myself to be, it is an expert. We have a lot to discuss about the expert label a bit later. I'll share my thoughts about being called a legend, a father/mother, or an expert of anything at length. But for now, to kick off the career guide that the entire self-improvement industry never knew it even needed, let me be crystal clear.

Not only am I famous with 12 people, but I'm also famous for something that, statistically and mathematically speaking, almost nobody on the planet cares about.

Billions of people walk this earth daily and never think about digital identity or cybersecurity. Thousands upon thousands are interested in what I'm known for, though. I'm not writing this book to be famous with 14 people. I'm not writing this book to become any more known than I am now. There is a distinct reason that I call this a career guide. I firmly believe that the stories, knowledge, and skills I share with you can and will dramatically and positively affect your career. If it all works out for you, that information should also dramatically and positively impact your personal life.

My inspiration to write this book came from a simple email exchange with people I care about and trust me. Naturally, they are people I want to help be successful. About two hours before I started tapping out the first words of the draft that would become this book, I emailed my staff at my current place of employment. I was the Chief Product Officer for a Round B start-up company in cybersecurity.

The topic I covered in the email was a request for a rapid media response for Information Week. For those who are reading this book and who don't work in technology, Information Week is a media channel for nerds—or techno-nerds. It is a pretty good "get" for a cybersecurity professional because Information Week covers more than cybersecurity. They cover all of technology.

I know; it is positively riveting, am I right?

My Chief Marketing Officer, Nicole Rowe, previously mentioned, had sent me the reporter's request, and I was writing a couple of sentences to send back.

I hammered out a set of responses to four questions about motivating your senior leadership to embark on a Zero Trust strategy. (It just keeps getting better and better, doesn't it?) I forwarded those responses to a few of our company's employees. It felt like the perfect moment to share "tips and tricks" as a part of their career development.

Nicole and I had a conversation a few days later about that decision. I will never forget her telling me, "I've never seen anyone do that before." At first, I wasn't sure what she meant. Nicole explained that she had worked with many of the biggest names and leaders in technology, and none had ever taken a moment to teach other people how to do what I had attempted to teach our team.

The discussion gave me a lot to think about. I realized that most people in the spotlight aren't naturally inclined to share it. Maybe it isn't a conscious decision, though. We get so consumed with our day-to-day lives that we don't necessarily think about how we can enable and empower others to do what we do. We likely don't even ask if they want to do what we do.

I shared the moment with the team because I thought several could contribute to rapid requests and speaking events. Building and developing more voices created more opportunities to spread the message for our company. Over that week of requests and conversations, I recognized that I had learned every skill and pointer I had collected over the past few years.

It struck me that if I had learned them, I could also teach them.

I'm writing this book for everyone who wants to learn how the magic of becoming a recognized personality, expert, or leader in their respective career disciplines happens. This book is for anyone who wants to understand the unwritten rules of how this strange and wonderful endeavor of being micro-famous works. Most of us have something important to share, but few know how to start. This book is written to serve as that starting point.

I've always been passionate about providing people who work within my team with the tools and support they need to be wildly successful. Hoarding what I've learned solely for personal or professional enrichment doesn't make sense. I've reached the pinnacle of my professional career. Maybe not the pinnacle in terms of years worked, as I still have a lot that I want to do and contribute within my profession. When I say pinnacle, I mean that I have reached a level in my career   I never anticipated. I could stop working tomorrow and feel like I had accomplished quite a bit.

I've held multiple "Chief" and senior executive titles. I've been part of the team that took a company public—standing on the New York Stock Exchange floor while the bell was rung. Whew, that was incredible! I've also worked in the hectic small start-up company world. There is nothing quite like experiencing the zoom-zoom highs of securing funding and booming sales growth, along with the heartaches of poor performance and terrible leadership.

In my former corporate life, I earned awards and delivered hundreds of millions of dollars' worth of projects and products. I met more titans of industry than anyone ever needs to meet. I have friends and former colleagues who are CEOs, founders, and "the most influential this" or "the creator of that" worldwide. I could hang up my professional cleats and jersey right now and be satisfied that I've had a hell of a career and a whole lot of fun.

With all this career success, I'm always humbled. I work hard to never forget that I'm just a fishing captain's son from a small town. There is no way that my beginnings could have predicted my career journey.

The difference maker for my entire life wasn't my talent or skills but what someone saw in me that I didn't see in myself, abilities I never knew I had.

The difference makers were leaders who showed me that almost everything in the business world is teachable. Fortunately, those difference makers also taught me that if you are a great leader, you know that your legacy is the people you help grow, learn, and excel. No matter what widget you created, how many people you've managed, or how many dollars you've made, the people you teach are your legacy.

What matters most is sowing into others to help them succeed. Helping others succeed has an exponential impact on one's growth and success.

I'm probably the least qualified person to make such a bold statement. Still, I'm glad to live in a time when many highly successful entrepreneurs, investors, business leaders, and cultural icons share my sentiments.

So maybe I am trying to be famous with more than 12 people. If fame, or micro-fame, is the conduit to teaching others how to be successful, I'll take it. Whether or not increased fame is the result of this book, my primary goal is to create a navigational guide to empower a worldwide army of micro-famous people who help the people in their community be more successful.

I can help you and many others expand your career so you, too, can be a strong voice or an expert. Not because it will most likely bring you more money, accolades, or status in society, but because you are passionate about what you know and have something to say. What you have to share is important if you've dedicated your life, focus, energy, and personal resources to being good at something. Even though I was motivated to write this book by a singular event with my staff, my commitment to writing it evolved to include you.

Let's get back to that airport email. In the process of providing feedback to my team on the methods I use to increase the chances that a reporter or writer will use a quote that I've provided, I realized that what I do now that has earned me the label "expert" isn't because of how smart I am. If that were the case, I wouldn't be famous with anyone. I'm not smarter than any other average bear.

The "how" of being looked at as an expert, industry voice, or an industry mover and shaker doesn't just manifest in someone genetically. It is learned. Since it is learned, it can be taught. This realization was the eureka moment for me. Being famous with 12 people, possibly being bestowed the honorific of "expert," and the mechanics of amplifying your message in a noisy world can all be taught and learned. I know I already shared that, but it is worth repeating.

I hope you are reading this book for what it is genuinely intended to be: a career guide. It doesn't come with a guarantee that these recommendations will result in you becoming a known personality. Timing and good fortune have a part to play as well. It would be disingenuous to tell you that becoming famous with 12 people has anything to do with luck.

Serendipity plays a role, but serendipity is not the same as luck. I'll explain the difference and why that difference is critically essential later. Also, if being famous with 12 people was mostly luck, this would be the shortest and least-read career development book of all time. Many of the tips I will share on these pages can still be positive and valuable learnings for your everyday job, even if you never once set foot on a stage or get interviewed on television.

For those who aspire to get on stage or get interviewed on television, huzzah! Many people feel they have what it takes to be a public speaker, an industry or community advocate, and a change agent. Most people simply have no idea how to get there. Getting there is way more than what you know, where you went to school, or, as many mistakenly believe – who you know. A network is essential, but your network isn't going to hand you a platform. This career guide will pull back the curtain and open the doors and windows that have remained locked. It explains how things work in this micro-famous world. And I hope it decrypts some of the mysterious unknowns for you.

Why do I minimize the influence of the micro-famous by saying, "famous with 12 people?" It isn't because I'm disrespecting those who are micro-famous or self-deprecating about my micro-fame level. I say "only 12 people" to keep the realities of micro-fame in perspective. I am not finding a cure for cancer. I am not saving human lives by running into burning buildings or upholding the law. I'm not serving on the front lines of any conflict. I'm simply sharing knowledge and expertise that I hope will help others on that same path.

I take my responsibility to be an agent for good very seriously. I feel passionate that my responses to media requests aren't only about my industry but also extend to keeping my parents, children, and friends safe in the digital world. I have been a part of critical national and global commentary on topics like election security, consumer rights, and the Russian invasion of Ukraine. My personal world is as important to me as the global community.

Often, when I'm asked to interview or speak, I think, "Really, you couldn't find anyone better than me?" It isn't imposter syndrome (which we will be talking about) that causes me to think that. Instead, I still feel like I'm a learner. I still have a lot to learn. Part of the responsibility, when you grow your audience and become micro-famous is to not become an ass about it by forgetting that you are not done learning.

If you grow a giant ego and display it as you become famous with 12 people, you won't be micro-famous for very long. There is no margin or tolerance for arrogance and entitlement when you choose to make a publicly facing persona for yourself in your industry. If you lead with ego, believe me when I share this one simple reality: no one will be interested in listening to you.

I want you to find your voice. Even more so, I want you to have the knowledge necessary to navigate all the mysteries of speaking, submitting calls for presentations, using social media of every variety, writing, speaking, engaging in meaningful conversations in your industry, and having a positive, healthy impact on the world and communities around you.

It is time to unravel the grand mysteries of how to become famous with 12 people!

WHAT MAKES YOU THE EXPERT?

———————

Who gets to decide if you're an expert — is it something you can claim, or is it earned? Is being an expert the same as being an influencer or a personality? Can you declare yourself an expert? In this chapter, we'll dive into what truly defines expertise and how it compares to influence and public presence.

———————

What is the difference between an expert, a personality, an influencer, and a celebrity?

The answer to that question, like so many of the great puzzles and queries in history is, it depends. It depends on who is asking the question. It depends on who is answering the question. It depends on whether you even care about the answer.

If you ask a young person today who or what an influencer is, they may have a specific definition that is informed, not just by their own opinions. The influencer ecosystem, which they are likely inclined to participate in, will have sway in their opinion.

If you ask someone with a long career with expertise in any industry, you might get a curmudgeonly muttered, "There are no experts," in response. Sometimes, if you ask someone, they'll tell you, "I'm the expert." It's a bold assertion, but is it true? With so many titles and terms for people representing some degree of professional importance to another person, it is easy to see why they get mixed up and misapplied regularly.

I'm confident that there are lengthy and vigorous debates in some coffee shops or on Reddit about whether So and So is an influencer. There are probably not many debates going on about whether someone is an expert or not. Which is funny when you think about it. Influencers are now so prevalent in our society we don't even question their existence. We argue about the degree of their influence and whether they've ascended to the title of "influencer." We don't have the same discussions about experts.

Experts are just experts. Either by being described by others or by qualifications required in many professions. When there aren't hard and fast requirements to identify someone as an expert, though, the debate begins. In those cases, who is and who isn't an expert is almost always foreshadowed by a simple question:

Who made you the expert?

You felt the emotional tinge to that question, didn't you? Even though it is written, you can feel the diversity of tones in which it is usually asked. That feeling probably doesn't exude a cheery, happy tone. I think it is helpful to tackle the other honorifics first before we put the term "expert" under the magnifying glass.

The career goals aligned with this book are squarely oriented towards being recognized as experts, so clarifying the other terms helps us understand how they all work together. And they all work together. Don't be fooled into thinking that there isn't at least an edge of "influencer" in the recipe for being seen as an expert.

Let's talk about personalities first. Personalities seem like the vague middle ground between expert and influencer. Or are personalities a class and category all their own? Can I be an expert and not be a personality? A personality but not an influencer?

Personalities are people widely known by the general public, usually for their style of engagement. That style could be literal, in the form of fashion or interior decorating. That style can be figurative in the form of presence or demeanor. Personalities are typically recognized precisely because they are distinctive. Someone with a known personality doesn't need to stand for anything or take a position on matters outside their specific brand.   They don't need a mission or a focus. They may have had one at one time or still do, but they are known best for just being. Of course, this standard has some exceptions, but it is a fair generalization.

When we look at micro-famous people across every industry, we can find people who we believe are experts but also great, big personalities. How they walk, talk, look, and deliver their message is uniquely distinct. For many people, that style is a distinguishing mark to remember the person who gave the profound speech, created the revolutionary model or earned the recognition bestowed upon them by higher powers within their industry. If we consider the scientific and technology communities, Neil deGrasse Tyson, Bill Nye, and Steve Jobs are fantastic examples of experts who are also personalities.

You don't have to present an amazing personality to be famous with 12 people. You certainly can if you choose to, but it is a conscious decision. However, if we consider the three examples I gave, combining expertise with personal branding (that's right, folks, spoiler alert for content ahead) can multiply your results. The conscious decision I'm referencing is the intentional creation or expansion of your natural personality through establishing a personal brand.

Neil, Bill, and Steve have personalities that have become synonymous with their personal brand. Each has a style, approach, and affectations rooted in who they are at their core. These components of their personal brand have nothing to do with the topics for which they are considered experts. And yet, these outward manifestations of their personalities have become just as influential in popular culture as their books, products, and ideas.

Neil wants people to fall in love with science and mathematics. Even if you are a great teacher, that is not easy. Neil's effusive and enthusiastic storytelling and his dogged determination to make astrophysics a relatable topic is his "brand." This guy wrote a book titled "Astrophysics for People In a Hurry." Additionally, Neil always shows up to an interview or speaking engagement with a vest, a tie, or both, visually referencing the cosmos in some way or another. Nobody pulls off a vest emblazoned with the planets and stars quite like Neil.

Neil is not the only one with a neckwear fascination. If I say, Bill Nye, there are only two logical responses. "The science guy" and "the guy with the bow tie." Bill's fashion choices are front and center in our brains when we think about him. A lab coat? With a bow tie. A sharp suit? With a bow tie. Bill's mission of teaching and sharing the joys of science with kids for decades has been amplified by his conscious choices about presenting himself. Many people don't know that Bill is an accomplished mechanical engineer and inventor. Or that his path to becoming the teacher and science commentator we know now started when he began moonlighting as a stand-up comedian, separate from his career as an engineer at Boeing.

Steve Jobs may be one of the most meticulous crafters and integrators of a personality with a personal brand we've ever seen. Steve used the power of metaphors extensively. Not just in his speaking style but as a core principle in his design philosophy. In his biography by Walter Isaacson, Steve stated, "Part of the reason we model our computers on metaphors like the desktop is that we can leverage this experience that we already have." [1]

I don't believe it is a coincidence that just like Bill Nye and Neil de-Grasse Tyson, there is also a sartorial aspect of Steve Jobs' personal brand. Clothing, hairstyles, accents, and many other physical manifestations are often the first things that come to mind about a familiar personality. Jobs is famous for his black turtleneck, Levi's jeans, and New Balance sneakers. For years up to his passing, he wore this same outfit, stating that it allowed him to apply his brain to decisions and ideas without wasting any thought on what to wear each day.

If I said "The Man in Black" out loud, there is a better-than-average chance that you'd know I was referencing Johnny Cash. Recognizing the powerful impression visual components can bring to personal brands can be another valuable part of your journey to becoming famous with 12 people.

---

1   Walter Isaacson, Steve Jobs (Simon & Schuster, 2011), 127.

For this career guide, a personality is someone who has developed at least some type of personal brand and intentionally grows and protects it.

The next definition we need to tackle is celebrity. Celebrity is a category we don't need to spend time on because celebrities aren't micro-famous. Celebrities tend to be macro-famous. Even a B-tier talent will usually have more followers, fans, and enthusiasts than any person who is famous with 12 people. Celebrity isn't a great platform for experts to pursue. Sure, some celebrities contribute things to society (both good and bad), but they are rarely regarded as experts.

Which brings us to influencers.

The word "influencer" might elicit an emotional reaction within you. Unfortunately, the rise of digital culture has given many people the impression that "influencer" is a four-letter word. But the act of influencing is as old as human civilization. Throughout history, humans have been avid consumers of accidental and intentional influencers. It is a shame that the internet has bruised the term because influencers are valuable to everyone.

The first influencer I followed was an amazing man. Whenever I saw him as a kid, I was excited to absorb what he had to share. He seemed to care about me. He wanted me to learn about the world around me, be a good person, and make new friends.

His name? Captain Kangaroo.

Bob Keeshan influenced tens of thousands, hundreds of thousands, of kids like me. I also listened intently to the guidance and stories from Shari Lewis and Lamb Chop. I was never into Mr. Rogers, mainly because the PBS station was impossible to pick up on our television set with the broken antennas and missing knobs. Yes, there was indeed a time before streaming and cable television.

Whether it is Bluey or Sesame Street, we humans are introduced to and follow influencers almost from the moment we can exercise personal choice.

The availability of an expansive, global platform on the Internet has created a world where more people can influence others. More people than ever can subscribe to and consume information from their favorite influencers. Weirdly, the digital machinery that enabled this more democratized access has also distorted the term influencer for many people.

I love influencers.

Kevin, Tom, Jenn, Norm, Roger, and Richard from This Old House have greatly influenced my DIY pursuits. Brian Krebs has influenced the way that I speak and think about cybersecurity. I'm obsessed with Clive, the Wood-Fired Oven Chef, and I try to make every recipe he shares on his YouTube channel. I have the same passion and fascination with Martha Stewart, Anthony Bourdain, and Maneet Chauhan.

Social media influencers teach me something new daily about managing my brand and online presence. Influencer strategies have been adopted and leveraged by many of my favorite organizations focused on improving the world. Influencers put in a lot of work, time, and effort regarding their brand. The downside is that the explosion of the influencer culture has caused people to lump everyone with an online or media-related brand into one big community of people you supposedly can't believe in.

There is an upside to it, though, and that is all the tools and venues that have grown to support the influencer community that experts can leverage to share knowledge. The internet created a platform for people to share a lot of nonsensical and unhelpful noise. Still, in doing so, it also made the world's most extensive knowledge-sharing network.

And knowledge sharing is what this "expert" world is all about.

Every expert I know is a teacher at heart. The experts who immediately come to mind are the most well-known practitioners of dynamic neuromuscular stabilization in the world (Richard Ulm) and one of the best-known personalities in active shooter defense for the everyday person (Aaron Janetti). There are an untold number of people I don't know who are the most recognized knitters, dog trainers, homebrewers, or souffle makers; every single one of them wants to share their knowledge to help someone else.

I'd caution anyone who rushes to judgment and says, "But yeah, then they start to monetize their recognition, and then they are just a sell-out," or any other such criticism that is supposed to invalidate the value of their expertise. This is a hollow argument. What industry personalities do to get their expertise broadcast into the atmosphere so it can be shared and learned doesn't come without a price tag. Expertise is, after all, a commodity.

It also bears considering that for every person making a living off being recognized as an expert, there are 1000 who are paying for the opportunity. Few folks in the FW12P world get big endorsements or paychecks from a marketing department. We buy our podcast gear and self-publish our books because the available market isn't big enough. Many of us give up vast numbers of dollars to publishers for the privilege of being represented by them. Instead of getting paid for what we do and know, we participate in bunches of unpaid speaking gigs or uncompensated podcast interviews.

Hosting costs, advertising, tech tools, and software expenditures come from our pockets. We may not be launching full-scale businesses with inventories and staff to manage, but don't think for a moment that if our recognition expands to a point where we get a bit of economic enrichment, we aren't going to take it or that we don't deserve it.

This isn't a complaint. For those who are investing their time in reading this book, remember why you are here. The book's subtitle isn't "How to Become Obscenely Wealthy and Famous with Everyone Around the World by Showing Off How Expert You Are." Becoming well-known in your area of expertise isn't about you. I know that sounds like a contradiction. Indeed, it is about what you know and how you acquired that knowledge, but you are a distribution point.

What worth and value is there in the knowledge you only keep to yourself?

Being recognized as an expert in your field is an honor. People you have never met following you and referencing you in their professional and personal endeavors is more than an honor. It is a bond of trust between you and everyone who looks to you or breaks the proverbial bread with you in your community of influence. When you break that trust, you won't be the expert anymore.

Expert is a title that is given, not self-declared.

There are many career fields where the title of expert can be earned. Whether through years of effort, study, or practice, though, even these experts aren't self-declared.

Throughout this career guide, you will repeatedly see that the real work you put in is keeping that bond of trust intact and growing it with your audience. Can you be an expert and untrustworthy? It is a rhetorical question because the answer to that is already ringing in your head, isn't it?

That trust is a delicate currency that you must diligently cultivate and protect. You are not an influencer, although you will undoubtedly influence. You are not a celebrity, although you may experience brief moments of joy, adulation, or praise that will make you feel like one. You are a personality, though; in that regard, you are uniquely stamped as a "one-of-one" original edition.

What makes you an expert?

The world and the market around you are what make you the expert.

Being granted the title of expert doesn't come with a scepter, a crown, and a mandate that everyone will listen to you, let alone agree with you. That simple question, what makes you the expert, comes with the emotional triggers we discussed.

I usually hear it before someone tells me why I'm wrong and not an expert.

That criticism comes with the title. It is inevitable. As sure as the sun rises in the east, someone calling you an expert will be followed almost immediately by someone stating you aren't one. In academia, doctoral candidates must defend the thesis they spend years researching. They are not granted doctoral status unless they successfully defend their thesis. Conceptually speaking, this applies to expertise. Although, believe me, you will be asked to defend your expertise more than once and often by far less qualified critics.

Consider that to be another honor. Specifically, it is an honor that will keep you humble if you receive it correctly. When you put yourself out there in the public forum, you must be prepared for criticism and opposition. If you think you can be famous with 12 people and not have detractors, you may need to pause right now and re-evaluate whether you want to add the component of micro-fame to your career journey. The types, levels, and volume of criticism will depend on your area of expertise. But it will forever be a part of your life on this path.

Let me share a personal story about how being recognized as an expert is a double-edged sword. The situation I share in this story still stings and probably always will. The story starts with a piece of advice.

Don't try to be famous with 12 people on Facebook.

Or Instagram. Or any other personal social media channel. Not because these channels aren't valuable (and they can have a role to play in helping you grow and expand your influence), but precisely because they are personal to begin with.

In 2020, I received a lot of requests to speak about election security. My informed experience in election security isn't lightweight. Beyond my cybersecurity background, I am also one of the few cybersecurity practitioners who have been elected officials. I have deep contacts and connections within election boards at the county and state levels. I also have an extensive knowledge of the primary voting machine manufacturers and a solid knowledge of electoral information technology operations at the county, state, and federal levels. I was even invited to testify about election security at the Colorado Statehouse. All of which led a few media outlets to ask me to share my thoughts. So, I did.

I shared many of these news stories and interviews on my professional social media platforms. The reception by the professional audience that followed me on those channels was universally positive and supportive. Then, I cross-posted those media quotes to my personal Facebook account. I thought it would be educational and helpful to friends, family, and anyone in the public arena who was bored enough to read my feed. There wasn't a single partisan sentiment in my comments or quotes. I only spoke about the components of election security that I knew and understood in detail. You already know what happened.

Here are just a couple of names that were directed at me.

Idiot.
Moron.
Talking head.

I was even accused of being a state-sponsored member of the agitprop and the "fake media." I'm not making that up. Someone in my large circle of personal friends used the actual word agitprop. What in the Cold War era hell? In their minds, I was a phony expert given a platform so that I could propagate misinformation among the masses. Want to know what it feels like to be called out as a traitor, a propagandist, and an idiot?

It hurts.

None of my experience or societally granted "expert" status that I enjoyed across a global group of followers numbering in the thousands mattered a single damn bit. It didn't matter that the people, friends, and acquaintances of friends who made those kinds of spot assessments were people with zero background or experience in election security. It didn't matter that no one had called them for their uninformed opinion on the topic or any other topics.

Not only were they not at their statehouses testifying, but they also hadn't even gone to their respective statehouses to protest or listen to a single word from the other experts lined up there. The fact that major news outlets carried my statements was irrelevant and only worsened their opinion of those comments. I was a sell-out. A charlatan. A flim-flam artist. I had conned my way into this mini-famous status.

People who criticized my observations used the question "Who made you the expert?" as a weapon. They assumed I was a self-declared expert and had faked my way into the news.

In no way does being a self-declared expert give you opportunities for these media quotes. You can't wing it when it comes to popular media. Professional journalism has standards and protocols like doctors and lawyers do. There are rules to qualify the experts they invite to their platforms for commentary on the news. So, the criticism that I or any other personality has "faked it until they made it" isn't remotely accurate.

When you work up to higher-visibility media outlets (usually culminating in broadcast media on major networks), you will never be invited back if you or someone else suggests you are an expert, but you aren't.

Whatever our opinions are about the media today, they don't have room for faux experts. Granted, some experts may have views that align with a particular media outlet's perspective, but none of these outlets are fools. They have their own brands and bottom lines to protect. They don't risk it on people pretending to be experts. The media will teach you a harsh lesson if you think it does.

This type of behavior is rampant only on personal social media channels. Consequently, there are virtually no rules about qualified expertise for social media pontificators versus guests on mainstream media platforms. There will still be criticism on professionally oriented channels or outlets, but it rarely turns ugly. I fear that might change as more people feel entitled to the strength of their uninformed opinions over the value of an informed opinion, evidence, data, or expert experience.

The best example I can offer you to distinguish influencers from experts is in stock market-related content. Suppose you search "stock trading advice" on any social media channel. In that case, you will be bombarded with ads from influencers pitching this trading app or that $7 trading course, each guaranteed to make you a millionaire overnight. If you peruse the finance section of any given major media outlet, you will find commentary and expert analysis from professionals in the industry.

Would you rather invest your money based on the advice of a TikTok day trader or an experienced analyst who appears on CNBC's Squawk Box broadcast?

For now, the best guidance I can offer is understanding that you are on a split-personality-journey when choosing to be famous with 12 people in your career. There is the professional you, and there is the personal you. The critical binding agent between those two personalities is that you look the same, and that's about it. Blending personal and professional personas isn't impossible, but many things must be considered before you attempt it. I recommend reading the rest of this book to understand the key components of being famous with 12 people before you make that decision.

Identifying as an expert can sometimes be tricky. Beyond a credentialed expert title, self-referencing as an "expert" should almost always feel weird. It should usually be a description of last resort.

I rarely make any claim to the expert title. On the rare occasions when I do, it usually is to shorten what would be a lengthy dissertation on my background and experience. Or, as an answer to the more probing and sometimes overly persistent question, "No, seriously, what is it that you do?"

I never claim to be an expert in the company of my peers. First, I consider it disrespectful to our collective expertise. Our respective communities of practice have thousands and possibly hundreds of thousands of thinkers, thought leaders, innovators, rabble-rousers, and change agents. Progress can and is frequently caused by an epiphanic "Shazam!" moment from anyone in our communities of practice. If you can't appreciate that the people around you can be instantaneous or temporal experts, you don't know anything about high jumping.

How's that for a transition?

High jumping is a fantastic example of why everyone in your community of practice and field of endeavor deserves respect and should not have to hear you prattling on about your expertise. Dick Fosbury is my favorite example of this truth.

Dick was in high school and frustrated by his high jumping performance. In 1963, he struggled to clear 5', the qualifying height required in Oregon high school track and field. He went to his coach and told him the standard and accepted straddle technique just wasn't working for him. He was going to try the scissor technique that nobody used anymore. His coach advised him not to, and the non-expert 16-year-old Fosbury didn't listen. Now for my favorite part.

Fosbury approached the bar, executed the less-than-desirable scissor technique, and made it over the bar but felt a sensation. The bar brushed his butt as he cleared it. In one "Shazam!" moment, Fosbury asked himself the question that changed an entire event and led to superhuman heights in the high jumping world. The question? "How do I raise my butt over the bar in the middle of a scissor jump?"

In his next jump, he started his scissor technique with his left leg, arched his back, lifted his hips, and instead of scissoring his right leg, he let it stay and hang in the position it was in. Folks, in one moment of self-introspection and determination, no one on the planet can deny that Dick Fosbury became a situationally enlightened expert.

It took Fosbury some time to perfect what he had discovered. He set his school record but came in second place his senior year at the State Championships at 6' 5.5". Yep. In two years, he had moved from being unable to clear the high school qualifying height to adding nearly a foot and a half to his personal best. He would continue to build his expertise in 1965 when he joined the Oregon State University track team. He went on to win the gold in the 1968 Olympics and set the Olympic record.

Now, you might believe this moment of enlightenment and several years of Fosbury Flop usage would have assured that the experts in high jumping had all changed course and were coaching their athletes to use it. But in 1972, the Olympic gold medalist used the straddle technique. In 1980, 3 Olympic finalists were still using the straddle. And Fosbury didn't break the world record in 1968 when Valeriy Brumel held it. Valeriy set that record five years before using the straight-legged straddle technique, and it would take until 1971 before the American Pat Matzdorf broke it. Matzdorf also used the straddle technique.

We might be eager to wave this example of spontaneous expertise away by suggesting that Dick Fosbury was a fluke. He wasn't an expert minted in a single moment; he just got lucky. But the tale of the flop is so much more interesting than just Dick's auto-discovery of a new jumping technique. Because 300 miles to the north of Dick Fosbury and at almost the same time in the 1960s, Debbie Brill intuitively discovered the same back-to-bar high jump method. Another instantaneous expert! Debbie set her first Canadian National high jump record in 1969 and broke her record multiple times until her final Canadian national record was established in 1984. That record still stands today, as it is one of the oldest unbroken records in all Canadian track and field.

I wonder, among the self-declared experts in the high jump in the 1960s, if Dick Fosbury and Debbie Brill would have been invited to share their thoughts? Without a doubt, many people in the world from the 1960s to 1980s considered themselves experts in the high jump. I bet they were adamant about what worked and didn't work regarding the high jump. They were the experts. However, a young man from Portland trying to find his way after his parents divorced and his brother died, as well as a young woman growing up on a farm in Western Canada, greatly impacted their community of practitioners. In reading about everything I could find on both, neither considered themselves experts.

Declaring yourself to be an expert doesn't make it so. Painting "expert" on the side of your personal branding bull horn and shouting it to the rooftops doesn't mean anyone will listen or acknowledge your noise. Be careful and guard your words when referring to yourself with the term. When Debbie Brill was asked if she ever thought that the Fosbury Flop should have been known in history as the Brill Bend, she shared this bit of wisdom.

"No, I have never felt that way. I'm quite happy with the way that it is. It doesn't matter that people don't know. I want to be great at what I do, but I don't care if I'm well-known for it. I think I might be happier for it."[2]

Spoken like a true expert.

While I don't have all the answers on who should or shouldn't be called an expert, I hope this chapter has helped you understand how to handle and manage that title yourself. Maybe "expert" won't ever be used in the same sentence as your name. And that is okay because you don't become an expert through some ceremony or ritual. You aren't anointed an expert because you declare it so. Whether you work in a field that offers a pathway to being a certified expert or in a profession where it is a title granted by your peers and the community, the inescapable truth is that "expert" is something you earn.

When someone asks, "Who made you the expert?" you should be able to confidently declare, "Not me." Then, you should be able to follow up with, "The market or my community recognizes me as someone who knows something about this thing." Turn the question into an opportunity to share knowledge.

Like Debbie Brill said, focus on being great at what you do.

---

2   Track and Field News March 1982

I WISH I COULD GET PAID TO TALK FOR A LIVING!

Do I really need to be a public speaker? Why is storytelling so much more powerful than just delivering a PowerPoint presentation? Isn't sharing the information enough? In this chapter, we'll explore why making a personal connection through storytelling is far more effective than data and graphs alone and how it can transform the way your message resonates with your audience.

The number one question I get from people about my career path is, "How do I get a job like yours?"

The number one statement I hear about what people think I do is, "I wish I could get paid to talk for a living!"

Ah, if it was only so easy as talking, we'd all get paid, wouldn't we? If you are a gifted talker or natural speaker, there is plenty of helpful advice in this chapter and others to help you get even better. But if you are terrified of opening your mouth to utter a single syllable, I have some excellent news for you! Everyone can speak in public!

I know, I know. You have a terrible fear of being on stage, on a podcast, doing an interview, or even speaking to a group of strangers in a hallway. It doesn't matter. I've met and worked with so many incredible speakers, and more than a few of them still have those same fears.

Your fear isn't an acceptable excuse for keeping what you have to share locked up inside of you.

Public speaking is like singing loud and clear for all the world to hear (thanks, Will Ferrell). I can't remember where I heard it said or saw it written, but I recall a brilliant observation about singing several years ago. Someone said, "I can't sing." A singer looked at them and said, "Can you talk?". The response was, "Yes, of course, I can talk." The singer responded, "Then you can sing. Singing is just talking but saying the words either longer or shorter."

I thought that was pure genius. I get that the singer was talking specifically about the mechanics of singing.   Even if you can sing well mechanically, you can keep time, and you are great at phrasing and breathing, you could still just suck at singing when it comes to things like being on-key. That is a totally different issue. Being able to sing and sing well aren't the same thing.

It's very much the same with public speaking. Everyone with a voice is capable of speaking. And mechanically, everyone can be a speaker. Maybe not a good speaker, but even that is fixable. However, there is one absolute surety about speaking: you can't be famous with 12 people without doing it.

This is why speaking is the very first growth topic of this book. You have a huge leg up if you are already a great speaker. If you are mechanically able to speak and want to be recognized as an expert in your field, you are on your way. However, if you are reading this and already stone-set on the belief that you can't speak in public, you may as well not finish reading the book. Yes, you must overcome the notion that you cannot speak publicly to become micro-famous in your field.

Albert Einstein once said, "Do not worry about your difficulties in mathematics; I assure you that mine are greater." That is a fantastic piece of wisdom that showcases Einstein's sense of humor. It isn't a humble brag if you are Albert Einstein, am I right? Einstein is right that our hardships, challenges, and hang-ups are relative. Which is why, when you dig your heels in and tell me, "Richard, you don't understand. I just can't speak in public", I'm going to say neither could Stephen Hawking.

And yet, he did.

Stephen Hawking did plenty of speaking in his early career as a professor and researcher. While he first learned at 21 years old that he had an incurable motor neuron disease, he didn't lose his voice until he had an emergency tracheostomy in 1985. He didn't let this stop him from finding a way to speak extensively over the next 33 years of his life.

Think about that for a moment. You probably have full use of your vocal cords. Yet you adamantly insist that you can't speak in public. Yet, you speak everywhere else. Are you starting to see the problem with your argument? Stephen Hawking wouldn't let the physical inability to speak keep him from speaking.

If you've never seen Stephen Hawking's presentations, take a moment and pull up any of his interviews or speeches online. Hawking wasn't just a great speaker but an incredible storyteller with a brilliant sense of humor. And he didn't even have his own voice. Without these speaking engagements, we wouldn't have a universe of Stephen Hawking quotes or his responses to in-the-moment events or feelings to understand his level of genius and our universe.

We would have to read all his books, papers, and musings to get the same understanding of the man as one single speaking engagement could provide. And it is fair to say that if Stephen Hawking hadn't continued to find his voice, we wouldn't know his name as we do today. Let's face it: a theoretical physicist with a side hustle in cosmology is the best example of an expertise that should make you famous with about a dozen people at best, and Stephen Hawking was very clearly a global superstar and celebrity.

I understand if you have an unresolvable fear of speaking in public. I'm not belittling or mocking that fear. This book isn't the best to teach you how to overcome that fear by a long shot. There are many great books on the subject, and I've heard repeatedly from people I cross paths with on the speaking trail that their journey to overcome that fear was to join an organization like Toastmasters. I have never been a member of Toastmasters International, but their approach makes perfect sense.

Public speaking is a skill. If you think about any skill for a moment, chess, gardening, bowling, or woodworking, practice makes you better. Toastmasters get you that practice and a healthy dose of guidance on structuring your speeches and finding your voice. Alternatively, you can choose the more challenging route and just dive into it. Regardless of your path, once you get rolling, you will get tons of opportunities to practice.

Casting aside (but still respecting) your objections to speaking out of the way, there are simple guidelines I will discuss later how to turn your professional speaking persona into your brand. However, the "what" of your speaking and how you do it is fundamental to adding FW12P to your career goals and path.

The first piece of advice? Nobody cares about your expertise level when you speak to them. So don't be an expert.

Sounds crazy, right? I'm writing a book to help you become a locally, nationally, or internationally recognized expert among your peers and maybe even more than just your peers. My first advice is, "Don't be an expert." It is almost like I'm trying to encourage people not to read this book. There is a method to this madness, though. Rest assured.

Yes, your expertise is important. I'm not discounting that fact. You've spent a lot of effort and time building it. But your expertise isn't more important than how you present it. After years of being famous with 12 people, I can confidently tell you that presentation is at least as important as knowledge.

If you have Beyonce-level presentation skills and presence, but your expertise is not genuinely earned, you will quickly be dismissed from the public square. Audiences are quick to judge. Conversely, you can be the sole expert in your field with no viable contenders. If you have the presentation and poise of a rock, you will be dismissed. No one will even listen.

You must learn to have the poise and delivery of The Rock, not a rock.

I have talked to many people who find this reality maddening. They believe you should be heard if you are a bona fide expert in something. They discount the plain fact that listening to someone is entirely optional. Humans don't and won't listen to things that aren't compelling, interesting, and phrased in a way that inspires them or speaks directly to the most important motivator for human behavior.

In other words, people want to know, "What's in it for me?" before they commit to hearing your message.

Many people can't even process your expertise unless you put it in a package that has personal meaning to them. Being the expert in the room isn't going to get you noticed. Many people, including the audience that is supposed to be interested in your topic, may be completely turned off by your level of expertise. They might even feel threatened by your expertise.

Three key components to speaking are at least as important and possibly more important than showcasing your expertise. They are:

- Storytelling
- Connection
- Humility

Think for a moment about something said by someone you follow in the "Famous with 12 People" category. I don't know who that is for you. It could be some elite but obscure athlete. Perhaps it is the head of one of the world's largest banks. Maybe you follow a surgeon with a well-known technique named after them. Do you follow them because of their unique, one-of-a-kind expertise in the topic you are interested in or passionate about?

Not at all.

You follow them not because of what they say but how they say it. This is a lesson that I learned as a kid from one of the best business teachers I have ever had: my dad. Everybody loves a great story!

Growing up on his fishing boat, I watched my father simultaneously entertain and educate thousands of customers through storytelling.

While it might seem quaint that my dad was a fishing guide, and you might assume that all fishermen naturally tell stories, you'd only be slightly correct. My father was a salesman to his core, one of the best I've ever known. At its peak, my father's charter fishing service was one of the largest on the Great Lakes, with a dozen boats and as many captains. He and my mom owned and managed accommodations for their customers long before there were enough hotels to support the volume of their business. Storytelling was fundamental to the growth of his business, and I learned the trade of walleye and smallmouth bass fishing, as well as creating compelling narratives from a master of both crafts.

Storytelling isn't about describing a scene. It is about reaching someone at an emotional level. A brochure or a website tells a story, but it isn't storytelling. The greatest storytellers pull you into a world or a setting that resonates with you. Then, that storyteller makes the critical connection between you and an important message or lesson. Storytelling is a tool used by the very best speakers in the world.

Waving your hand at bullet points on a PowerPoint presentation or reading from the slides isn't and never will be storytelling. As any of us who have sat through hundreds, if not thousands, of meetings can testify, we have all suffered through enough bullet points and status updates.

Another helpful contribution storytelling provides when speaking and presenting is that it gives you a safe anchor to maintain your focus. The stories we develop to explain critical points or themes are easier to remember. They are easier to remember because they have emotional context and interest for us, just as they do for our listeners and audiences. We are attached to these stories, literally and figuratively. If you struggle with nerves, anxiety, and fear, building your presentation around a story is incredibly useful. If you lose focus on your points and message, you can reorient yourself to the story and get back on track.

We are usually actors in the stories we create, which helps us keep them straight. Even when we craft stories about something that happened or we were associated with, and we aren't one of the main characters, stories still have a sticking strength in our brains that we can use to our advantage.

The most significant value of stories in your speaking engagements is that they are the entry point for connectedness with our audience. Telling a great story doesn't guarantee any degree of connection with the people hearing it, but stories can't be beat as a starting point.

I'd like to share one of the most powerful stories I've ever told regarding audience reaction.

A couple of years ago, I had the opportunity to give a keynote presentation that more than 1,000 people would attend. While preparing for the engagement, I started thinking about my frustrations with connecting with my audience on the topic in the past. Everyone I discussed the issue with agreed it was a massive problem in the corporate world, but I never felt the audience was with me when I was talking about that problem.

I don't mean booing or tomatoes were thrown at me onstage. As I hit the key points in my presentation and looked out at the audience, I saw the doleful nodding of heads in unison. I saw an audience that acknowledged the problem but registered an emotional engagement that said, "Yes, you are right, and we are all suffering together in silence because of this problem."

I didn't get much satisfaction out of watching people, in the words of my friend Dr. Chase Cunningham, agree that we were all simply enjoying "the self-licking ice cream cone of misery." I realized my audience cared about my presentation but wasn't emotionally engaged.

While the problem I was speaking about is specific to what I do for a living, I know you'll understand its importance. Everyone faces horrible problems related to their digital identity in the digital world.

Everyone has online accounts, passwords, logins, and personal information that the bad guys constantly steal.

The problem statement was simple: Almost all companies on the planet fail to discover that the bad guys are in their systems until after they have already stolen all your data—and yes, I mean your personal data.

Many people outside the technology and security world assume that the good guys are great at stopping the bad guys in the digital world. The truth is that many of the companies you do business with are awful at knowing when someone who is not supposed to be in their digital systems is in their digital systems. If you ever want to hear more on the subject, just Google "Richard Bird" and the word identity, and you'll find plenty to keep you occupied.

My problem in past presentations was that there was not a deep, visceral link between the data and identities that my audience and I were supposedly protecting. There was also no urgent need to do anything about it when things went wrong. The story that changed that and became a talking point used by many people in my field forces people to face the uncomfortable truth about our failure to understand the actual consequences of not urgently caring about strangers inside our digital systems.

When I took the stage, I started with all the required preliminaries. I introduced myself, relayed my background, and explained why I was passionate about helping solve the problems that everyone in the audience had. I said that one of our biggest problems was that we treated the digital world as magical and somehow different from our analog or "real" world.

I continued setting the table for my story. I reminded everyone in the audience that the digital world represents our everyday world, and that technology is a means of production. Technology isn't magical; it's just a faster tractor. Then, I asked the critical question to set up my story.

"How many of you in the audience today have a school-aged child? A child somewhere between kindergarten and the 12th grade?"

60% to 70% of the audience will typically raise their hands.

"Excellent! I'm a father of 6 myself. I am not just a technologist or a cybersecurity practitioner. I have also been an elected official. Before anyone gets worried about this political party or that political party, I'd like to emphasize that I was a nonpartisan elected official. I served on the board of one of the larger school districts in Ohio. I truly enjoyed serving on the board with amazing people who weren't just colleagues but friends. The school district I served for was big: more than $200 million for an annual budget, 42 school buildings, 116 buses, and more than 1600 staff and teachers.

I'd like you to participate in a thought experiment with me.

I want you to imagine that the school your child attends is your favorite school ever. You love everything about that school. You love your child's teacher. The office assistants. The janitors. You love your school's principal. One morning after you've seen your child off to school, at about 10:00 am, your cell phone rings, and it is one of those automated calling systems with a recording of your favorite office administrator at your child's school.

The recorded voice on the other end of the line says, 'We would like to inform you that there is a stranger in our school building. We do not know how long the stranger has been here. We don't know if their intentions are good or bad. We don't know exactly where the strangers are inside our building, and we don't know how they got in, how long they intend to stay, or why they are here. We don't know where they are going next in the building. But everything is okay. It's cool. Thank you and have a great day!'

A show of hands right now; who feels good about that message?

No hands: I don't see a single hand up.

Quick, just yell out, what do you do when you receive that call?"

From the audience, I hear, "I'm calling my kids' cell phone."

"I'm texting my child's teacher."

"I'm driving to the school immediately."

What an incredible difference between shouts from the audience and a bunch of sleepy heads nodding in unison! As this swell of energy came toward the stage, I asked the binding question.

"How many of you today in your companies react with the same urgency and emotion when a stranger is inside your digital systems?"

Silence. It wasn't the kind of silence created by boredom or disinterest. It was an embarrassed silence. The silence told you, "Oh, I've never thought about it like that."

"So, I know how uncomfortable that story makes you when I tell it. It makes me uncomfortable just sharing it. Do you have the same emotional response to bad guys and enemies inside of your companies' technology systems? These bad guys are trying to shut your company down, steal from you, disrupt your services, take airplanes out of the sky, stop life-saving surgeries, shut off entire power grids, and create fear in your community. Isn't that worth getting emotional about?"

The story I told had meaning for almost everyone in the room, not just the parents of kids. The other audience members had children and were all grown or had nephews, nieces, and other family members they cared about. And everyone in the room understood the risk of the unknown.

Maybe the person in the school who couldn't be identified had entirely honorable intentions and was a good human. But there was no way to know since the stranger in our school had not followed the necessary processes and procedures to gain entry, announce themselves, and declare their intentions.

Engagement in that story isn't just exemplified by raising hands and nodding heads. It is at the most profound personal level, at the level of our fears, love, concerns, and commitments to our children.

The emotional connection in that story is visceral. People "feel" something as they participate in the thought experiment. Using that feeling to make a correlation between what you are trying to convince your audience of or share with them and moving them to action is a powerful combination.

From my perspective as the teller, this is a fun story to tell. The audience wasn't expecting me to shift gears from "the best school ever!" to "there's an immediate threat I need to address." Seeing the audience's physical response to the tale made it fun.

That seismic shift between sunshine and storm clouds is an extremely powerful agent that brings emotions to the surface. Adding a call to action, "What are you going to do right now?" cements the connection between how the audience feels and what the audience members feel they need to do about it.

We all have stories accumulated across the different ages and stages of our lifetimes. Usually, we share those stories like our grandparents or great-grandparents used to share vacation pictures on the slide projector when guests came over for supper. We treat them like moments in time that have entertainment value.

Suppose you consider your adventures, mishaps, and victories as storytelling tools. In that case, you can make the correlations and associations with your passions and profession that drive an emotional connection to you and your presentation.

The best speakers can simultaneously ignite more than one emotional response and connection from their audiences. This is why being funny isn't the same as being a storyteller. Being amused can easily happen in isolation. A joke is funny. But social commentary can both amuse me and repulse me. Your uncle telling a lame joke at the dinner table isn't storytelling. John Stewart or Jerry Seinfeld exploring a situation or setting and then wrapping it up with a punchline? That's storytelling.

When it comes to connection, invoking multiple feelings with one story is a goal state. I connect with my audiences this deeply, one out of every four or five speaking engagements. It is such an advanced talent and technique that I can assure you that even though I understand it, I can't yet invoke it as well or as often as I would like to. It takes time and practice.

Connecting at a meaningful level with your audience also requires relevance. The story must be relevant to the needs and expectations of the people you are talking to. Asking a large audience how many of them have kids in school is a lay-up. You know the probability that many of them will be parents with young children is high. But, for a moment, think about how awkward it would have been if no one raised their hand, and I just proceeded with that story anyhow. People would be confused, and there would be no connection at all.

That scenario seems highly unlikely, but I always see it happen in terms of industry-specific expertise. A speaker asks the audience, "How many of you have experienced x?" No hands go up. The speaker then proceeds at light speed to spool out a story their audience has just informed them that is irrelevant to their needs or interests.

There can be many reasons for how this situation transpires, but I've mostly experienced it because the speaker did not do any research on the audience they were speaking to.

Your profession may be different from one where emotional engagement seems logical or achievable. Mathematics. Physics. Cardiology. Pet care. Plumbing. Sculpture. Auto repair. The wonky details and intellectual minutiae of our professional endeavors might be dry, mechanical, tactical, or just plain dull. You'll unlikely find comedy gold or heart-tugging stories of warmth in your explanation of AI algorithms, heart valve replacements, or kiln temperatures.

Yet, you can find those emotional connection points in your stories and how you relate them to your subject matter.

Diving into deep technical waters or speaking from an engineering or architecture diagram should be your approach only when you are 100% certain that most of your attending audience is on that wavelength. Cracking jokes during a presentation on a grave-serious topic might not be your best approach. Make sure that you've dug into the details of who you will be speaking to and considered where you are speaking. Do your homework about cultural differences if you are presenting far from home. If the answer to the question "What is important to the audience you are speaking to?" is "I don't know," that is a recipe for disaster for you personally and professionally. It is an inexcusable recipe, at that. Use your resources.

Ask your conference organizer. Search out colleagues who have spoken at these events before. Look up individuals on the attendee list to understand their backgrounds. Preparing to speak isn't just rehearsing your lines but also knowing your audience, knowing what material and equipment you need ahead of time, and knowing strange nuances such as "Does this conference allow me to use animations in my presentation slides?"

Yes, that is something you must prepare for ahead of time.

If you don't take the time to understand the nature of your audience, you could end up looking out over a sea of blank stares. What plays in Manhattan in the financial district might not play in Peoria at the meeting room in Alexander's Steakhouse. Be conscious of the geographical, national, cultural, and micro-cultural differences of the potential audience you are speaking to.

From personal experience, what sounds great in Dallas might not click down the road in Austin. If you speak internationally, don't talk about American football at great length to save some confused looks. Speaking of football, understand your room when giving some great sports-related analogy. Touting the legends of Ohio State or Alabama while speaking in Ann Arbor or Baton Rouge can lead to some awkward moments. Connection takes planning, focus, and a command of your audience.

As Deadpool says, believing a connection happens for lucky souls with great personalities is lazy writing.

Another aspect that distinguishes the ho-hum presenter from a stellar speaker is humility. This is yet another counterintuitive expectation. The common belief is that a speaker needs to be out front doing their dance. The center of attention is the only position public speakers are interested in on the stage. Personalities and experts must be egotists. Right?

Nope. Not really. Like, not even close to really.

Of the large number of personalities in cybersecurity that I hang out with, I don't know of one of them who is an egotistical, narcissistic attention seeker. Usually, they are the exact opposite. Quietly introverted in social settings or a small group and rarely inclined to loud, showy braying and dissertations on how important they are and how much they know. In a "never meet your heroes" moment, I had the opportunity to sit down and converse with someone I have followed for a long time. That person is the rare exception to my observation above. They are the singular exception.

What turned me off when I met this person I had such high regard for?

"I created this!"

"I have these many patents!"

"That guy stole my idea."

Our discussion was their version of me, myself and I. It was not a shock, but 12 months later, I was conversing with several colleagues at a dinner, and this expert's name came up. The group's lack of respect and interest in this person manifested instantly. One comment nicely summed up the dinner conversation: "I don't find value in someone who says that everyone in the world is doing it wrong, and they are the only ones doing it right."

A great English word for this characteristic is boorish. A boor is an ill-mannered person. And it is the height of ill manners to declare yourself an expert and then suggest that you are surrounded by a world filled with amateurs. Dick Fosbury and Debbie Brill are just two small examples of the temporality of expertise.

It's the right time, right place, and right idea. Being humble is easy for people who have been labeled experts. We must remember that the title was granted to us and can be taken away. Believing we are the singular expert on anything is ridiculous and obnoxious.

Humans seek out experts but don't want to be reminded that they are listening to an expert every moment. Exercising humility is easy, and it should be the muscle you exercise the most frequently. Acknowledge others in your field by name. Seek them out and ask how you can help them in their efforts. Collaborate with them. An expert is only effective in a healthy ecosystem of peers, colleagues, and friends.

We will revisit humility when we discuss authenticity, connecting with your audience, and disarming your critics. Being humble isn't just an act, even though you may need to make a conscious decision to be more gracious, thankful, helpful, or kind. But it is an aspect of being famous with 12 people that will come up repeatedly in your journey.

You don't have to be a great storyteller before you explore the edges of this new facet of your career. You don't have to be the world's best speaker. Being "okay" is the first step on this trail for you. But wanting to tell your story isn't the same as being able to tell your story.

You might be in a corporate situation that tactically limits your abilities by policy or practice. But if you are passionate about sharing, you will find a way. And when you find that way, you might unintentionally become famous with 12 people. Because, as you will soon find out, pursuing fame and recognition isn't about you, and you can't control it. It's about what you give.

Storytelling, connection, and humility are our starting points. Speaking and presenting effectively is so important that I want to take time in the next chapter to cover the topic more personally. We haven't dug into the most challenging part of speaking yet—your fear. So, let's get unafraid.

SECRET SAUCE - SPEAKING TIPS & TRICKS

Should I picture my audience in their underwear? Can you learn to be a better speaker? And what exactly is a muse, anyway? In this chapter, we'll debunk common myths about public speaking, explore how you can improve your skills, and uncover the role of inspiration in delivering compelling presentations.

Storytelling is powerful and fun, but many ways exist to become a more effective speaker and presenter. In this chapter, I will discuss muses, handling criticism, overcoming fear, and whether you should or shouldn't imagine that people are in their underwear.

What I've learned after speaking hundreds of times doesn't remotely cover everything that there is to learn. I am happy to share the knowledge I've acquired, but there are great teachers for you to consider.

Some fantastic resources exist that go into much greater depth and breadth on speaking, like the legendary "The Art of Public Speaking" by Dale Carnegie. The book was first published in 1915 and is still one of the most popular guides about public speaking ever written. For a more contemporary take on becoming a better speaker, Carmine Gallo's "Talk Like Ted: The 9 Public Speaking Secrets of the World's Top Minds." Carmine gives us a look into the heads of some of the world's best speakers, and that perspective is very useful.

While I'm not yet at that world-class TED level of speaking, I did want to take the time to share some of the more interesting insights I've accumulated about effective speaking. There are a few public speaking tips that I've gathered that are worth exploring and, in the case of fear, worth conquering.

The leaping-off point for this chapter is visiting the power of a muse as a contributor to our speaking style and presentation success.

Recently, I advised a friend on how to improve their connection with their audience. I asked her to identify her muse. I'll admit that this is a rare question these days. We don't often think about muses as influencing our lives anymore.

Yet, muses exist all around us in dramatic and positive manifestations.

A muse is the little bit of lightning in a bottle that steers the expression and phrasing of your ideas. It is a powerful contributor to creating a personal brand, recognizable voice, and differentiated perspective on communicating to the broader world. A muse is like tuning into a wavelength that clarifies your thoughts and expands your thinking on connecting with the world around you.

Unique and sometimes weird phrases, analogies, metaphors, and comparisons are significant components of my speaking style. Over the years, I've gotten a lot of questions about how I come up with these memorable bon mots. For a very long time, my response was, "I don't know; they kind of just jump out of my head."

While writing this book, the question came up again at a conference I spoke at. So, I sat down and thought about it for a bit. I realized that my speaking style and methods were greatly influenced by music. In response, I wrote a LinkedIn article explaining my muse and how it has been a crucial part of my public persona.

I hope sharing it here will inspire you to find that wavelength in your speaking endeavors.

CYBERSECURITY AND JOE STRUMMER

Many people ask me how I come up with so many unique and off-the-wall comments, quotes, and analogies about cyber-security, breaches, and exploits. I recently watched a trailer for a documentary about Joe Strummer called "The Future is Unwritten." It made me realize that I probably needed to share my personal secret about why my perspective on cybersecurity is both industry-divergent and so frequently picked up by the media.

I'll give the attention-challenged, or what the kids call the TL; DR: simply put, it's a revelatory moment that unlocked the punk ethos that is my core motivation.

Buckle up; you've been advised that this is more of a manifesto than a Tweet... er, X... er... whatever.

The original punks in music might just be Woody Guthrie, Johnny Cash, Bob Dylan, Miles Davis, John Coltrane, Charlie Parker, and Peter, Paul, and Mary (Pete Seeger, Mary Travers, and Paul Stookey). You can tell right out of the gate that I'm already sorting out the music listeners from the music fanatics. Still, even if you aren't deep down the rabbit hole in your own favorite music genre, hang on for the ride with me because I'll cover a whole lot of artists.

Punk ethos.

This is the tie that binds for me. For most people, "punk" equates to loud, fast, and angry. Fortunately, I was given an amazing opportunity to discover punk in its earliest and rawest forms before realizing it.

I was eight years old when I picked up my first saxophone. I'll tell you more about that in a moment.

I grew up in Lakeside, Ohio, a tiny community on the shore of Lake Erie. While for many with the same upbringing, that could mean a lack of access to the arts, that wasn't the case for me. Lakeside is one of the last remaining Chautauquas in the world.

What's a chautauqua, you ask? It's a 150-year-old American concept built around self-enlightenment, self-improvement, education, and community. There used to be hundreds of them in America. Methodist, Lutheran, Catholic, Spiritualist – they were structured summer camps that had educational and en-richment programs. You pitched a tent, and you learned, had fun, and made friends. I lived in one all year round.

Side note: In 1915, traveling Chautauquas visited over 12,000 American communities. Today, I know only three remaining communities in America: an ungated Chautauqua in Boulder,

Colorado, an ungated camp in Chautauqua, New York, and the gated one I grew up in Lakeside, Ohio.

We had an entertainment program every night for ten weeks in the summer, seven days a week. Growing up in this community meant my childhood experiences included seeing Victor Borge, The New Christy Minstrels, Three Dog Night, Ferrante & Teicher, and literally hundreds of other musicians and bands. If you don't recognize any of these names, that's okay. For a moment in time, many of these performers were at the top of the charts or had huge cultural impacts in the 40s, 50s, and 60s.

They were acts that stopped on the way between Vegas and the Catskills from spring to summer to perform in Lakeside's 3000-seat auditorium. Victor Borge is still one of the most impressive performers I've ever seen. My 7- or 8-year-old self can still picture parts of his act like it is a movie I replay every now and then. He had a magical impact on me and a lot of other kids back then. My favorite gag was when he would stop his piano playing, stand up in his full concert tuxedo, and pull a seat belt out of his piano bench to buckle himself in and continue playing.

Between that environment and living in an extended family where summertime singalongs with organ accompaniment were a near nightly event, it was inevitable that music would become my drug of choice. My mother plays the organ as well as my grandfather once did.

Back to picking up the saxophone at eight years old. So, it's 1975, and disco is starting to explode. Horn sections are coming back into popularity after the rise of various strains of rock and roll with The Beatles, Zeppelin, The Band, and Crosby, Stills, Nash, and Young. I'm completely entranced. However, as a young saxophonist, I'm also a bit bored because there aren't a lot of sax solos on those disco records. I was just born with a hyper-drive for intellectual curiosity. So, I asked my music teacher (love you, John Nuss) who I should be listening to. That question opened the door for me to the world of jazz.

Jazz, when it comes to saxophonists, is an interesting genre. We see a sax, and we think "jazz." But saxophones weren't the big instrument of the day at the beginnings of jazz in the Big Band era. Jack Benny wasn't a saxophonist; he played clarinet. Saxophones were more like the French horns of the early Jazz Age. Rich tones but always a supporting player to the whole ensemble. When the collision between jazz and blues eventually unfolded, a host of players began to pop up. Cannonball Adderly, Charlie "Bird" Parker, the still amazing (and one of the last survivors at 93 years old) Sonny Rollins, and the end-all-be-all John Coltrane himself. It was an awakening for me as a child before my tenth birthday.

I might be the only nine or 10-year-old who ever listened to Miles Davis's "Sketches of Spain" on repeat. Because this story can only be so long, this is where I time-hop. I rapidly ate up all the classic recordings of the saxophonists I mentioned earlier and dug into some more (like I said, down the rabbit hole). In this space, I discovered the avant-garde era of jazz. It was impossible for me to tell at the time that "Sketches of Spain" and Coltrane's "Giant Steps" were recorded just 17 years before I listened. To me, they were otherworldly and seemingly prehistoric. These jazz masterpieces were an unexpected gateway drug into a much broader world of counter-culture music.

And just like that, it was 1978.

As a listener and a poseur trying in my best adolescent form to imitate Coltrane, I think "thunderstruck" is an insufficient word to describe what it was like the first time I heard The Clash. I was instantly smitten. To me, there was a direct connection to Miles and Coltrane and Joe Strummer and Johnny Lydon and later to Jello Biafra and Henry Rollins. Don't even get me started on the still incredible synthesis of traditional and punk music that was The Pogues. Shane McGowan, in all of your glorious messiness, you are still and always will be one of the superheroes in my personal pantheon.

I haven't gotten to the revelatory moment yet. I've barely even scratched the surface of the fuel that drives my own creativity in cybersecurity. Perhaps you can see the mind map starting to unfold.

As I navigated through my early life using music as my compass, my path took a huge divergent turn on the road less traveled. I became a teenage parent. Those experiences and lessons are an entirely different essay for an entirely different time. The reality I faced then shut down my direct interaction with music for decades. I was still an avid listener who accumulated an untold number of artists and bands in my mental library. However, putting food on the table and navigating the joys, tragedies, and challenges of all-too-young parenting took me out of the fast lane. I became more like a librarian of music in the ages that followed.   Where exactly did I hit my revelatory moment?

After a family tragedy shattered everything I had known for almost a quarter century, a window of opportunity manifested to directly engage with the music scenes I craved as a kid. I went to my first music festival at the ripe old age of 50. On a Thursday night in 2016, my then-girlfriend Marie and I sat *down to a charity dinner at Bonnaroo. We happened to be seated next to Bob Ferguson. I didn't know at the time that Bob was the Creative Alliances & Music Outreach Project Manager at Oxfam. Bob, I have no idea if you remember this conversation or me at all. It's okay either way because epiphanies don't need to be bi-directional; just know that you opened my eyes in a way that changed the entire trajectory of the last seven years for me.*

As Marie, Bob, and I are talking, Bob begins to unravel his role and background. He came out of the corporate world of banking, just like I had. Bob spent his time working and interacting with every artist and band you've ever heard of to further Oxfam's charitable mission. I was in awe. I could have met the godlike form of David Bowie himself at that moment and not have been more enthralled.

In my sad, non-self-actualized self-pity, I looked at Bob and said, "Man, I'm just embarrassed. I grew up as the kid who ate punk music like it was pop-tarts, and now I'm just a corporate suit grinding out Excel spreadsheets with my headphones on and Rage Against the Machine turned up to 11. I'm a complete sell-out."

Bob looked at me and said, "At some point, we grow up and realize that you can't change the system from the outside. You've got to change it from the inside."

Shazam.

I didn't stop thinking about what Bob said for the entire festival. You combine that kind of epiphany with 24/7 bass drops, banjos, metal guitars, rap, and a healthy dose of 97 other types of music, and then you realize you've got some changes to make.

From that day to this, I opened all those dusty libraries of music and rabbit holes that I had explored in my younger years. The Talking Heads catalog sounded different, and the meanings of the songs just roared at me. My borderline unhealthy obsession with The Beastie Boys became a leaping off point to a recollection of early 90's NYC hardcore with acts like Orange 9MM and Helmet.   You can't dig into Chaka Malik and Orange 9mm without digging out the vinyl/cassette/digital downloads of Bad Brains. Bad Brains in 1978 or 1979 takes this kid right back to 11 and 12 years old, onward to the Black Flag era, and even further to the Henry Rollins years. The thick layers of genre-specific popularity can be peeled back like an onion for as long as you are willing to peel.

Clearly, every strain of punk rock music has been this decades-long boiling foundation for my worldview. Letting it free opened my mind up to the possibility of "telling the man" how it really should be while also, in some part, being the man. The punk ethos and its messenger, Bob Ferguson, tapped on my shoulder and said, "Hey man, you've been on the inside for longer than you've been on the outside by double – what are you going to do with that?"

I told that little voice, "I'm going to f**k some sh** up." Figuratively, folks, not literally. Let's keep this stream of consciousness in its appropriate metaphysical frame, shall we?

All too often, counter-culture artistic output is mistakenly conflated with anger. I've never processed it that way. To me, counterculture and anti-establishment art is about questioning systemic authority and asking, "Why not do this thing better?" That is the punk ethos. "Why are we not doing better?"

Considering the vast resources at our disposal, specifically the ubiquitous access to nearly infinite knowledge at our fingertips, why do we not do better? We possess more collectively accessible information than any previous generation of the human race, and we use it to share cat videos, watch porn and pontificate about our biases.

Punk ethos demands to know why we do not choose to do better. Why do we not do better than fascism? Why not better than capitalism? Why do we not do better than communism? Why have we not chosen better than racism, sexism, classism, ageism? The list of things we could and should be doing better in the 21st century is enormous.

As this deep need for music swelled in my life again, I realized that punks are everywhere. Johnny Cash? The man recorded a monument to anti-establishment music in – FOLSOM PRISON. If that isn't on the top 5 list of most punk things ever in human history, there is no punk. It's all a lie.

Peter, Paul, and Mary, Dylan, and way before them – Woody Guthrie – created folk music with a purpose. The NYC folk uprising in the 1950s was a socio-cultural awakening. Woody Guthries' "This Land is Your Land" isn't a patriotic anthem, people. It is a protest song. Getting a bajillion Americans to sing along to a protest song? That is peak punk territory right there.

What's more, the man did it in 1944! Do you recall I mentioned Coltrane and Miles Davis? By 1920, jazz had been banned by dozens of communities across the United States. In a wild irony, jazz was banned by New Orleans public schools in 1922 because it was "the devil's music." That ban wasn't abolished until 2022! Is jazz not scandalous enough for you? Hold my beer and watch this.

Need something more contemporary? How about those Wes Anderson movies, The Lego Movie or Thor: Ragnarök? Let's not forget The Rugrats! Now, I invite you to process that one of the Devo founders (yeah, Devo, the new wave/punk/art rock band that may have written the only song ever inspired by a Thomas Pynchon novel) has been sneaking subliminal messages to us mutants for decades through these movies. God bless Akron, Ohio, along with the Mothersbaugh and Casales brothers.

It's like Buzz Lightyear is wrapping his arm around Woody and saying, "I see punks. Punks are everywhere."

Punk ethos in music and pop culture is my personal philosophical treatise. I don't expect anyone to know any of the artists I've mentioned. If you do, I don't expect any of you to engage in labored efforts to show me where I may have mixed metaphors, timelines, albums, or acts. I only ask you to consider what your muse is that will force you to share your voice. What you have to say matters. What you've learned and experienced matters. It isn't what you echo along with the crowd that moves the needle. Or highlights injustice. Or right wrongs. Or create the change that you want to see or be. To accomplish this work, you must speak from your conviction. Your conviction is born from your muse.

Whatever that muse is for you, I hope you find your inner punk. Your muse may not be telling you to ask, "Why not better?" like mine did. For me, the punk that was buried deep down inside and hidden in a small town, the US Army, and the halls of cor-porate America doesn't need to be hidden anymore.

Because of my muses, I'm not going to stop finding ways to re-state the obvious, call out injustice, call those who should be called to account, hold those who are failing to be good stewards up to the light and demand "Why not better?" every single time I can. Because it isn't just me – it's an army of punks by my side. Together, we follow the army of punks that came before us.

Rock on.[3]

The response to this piece has been incredible. I received dozens of notes and messages from people who found their inspiration in music, saying they had forgotten about this band or that song. Others sent messages to convey how a particular singer still has profound relevance for them. Some folks told me about their muses, from athletes to historical figures to their grandfathers who served in WWII.

The concept of a muse, something or someone who inspires you to great heights, dates back almost 3000 years. The muses inspiring me to write, speak, and present like I do today were discovered when I was barely 12. While the edges of their inspiration could be occasionally seen in some of my work during my corporate career, it wasn't until I started speaking publicly almost 40 years later that the full force of their influence would spill out.

Content is only part of the equation for the best speakers in the world. Personality, context, connection, storytelling, and creativity are essential components of crushing keynotes, panels, and webinars. The muses accumulated throughout your lifetime will shape

---

3   Modified from the original for clarification. Published on LinkedIn August 18, 2023. https://www.linkedin.com/pulse/cybersecurity-joe-strummer-richard-bird/

your speaking style and delivery. As we grow older, we absorb the sources of these inspirations into our subconscious.

I encourage you to think about who or what those influences are for you and to dig back into them. Pull out those old records (or digital downloads). Crack open that old Steinbeck novel you have kept for no apparent reason since college. Listen again to those incredible speeches given by the master orators of today or from history. Watch those videos of Steve Jobs talking about great design principles. Visit one of Frank Lloyd Wright's masterpieces.

A minor downside of my Joe Strummer piece is that many people think musicians are my only muse. My muses are not limited to music, punk rock, or otherwise. I find inspiration in significant figures from history and writers with a keen sense of humor and a knack for observation. The personalities that inspire me share a common characteristic; they all tend to view our world from a slightly different perspective than everyone else around them. I'd like to think I also share this quality with my muses or at least try to exercise that same characteristic.

Albert Einstein, Mark Twain, and Will Rogers are just three examples from a sizable list of historical figures and authors who have influenced my writing and observation of the world around me.

Instead of the pop culture icon with his tongue stuck out and wild hair in full effect, Einstein the man is a constant fascination for me. His well-documented intellectual curiosity constantly reminds me to be intellectually curious. I use his coined term "thought experiment" all the time.

One of Einstein's most famous thought experiments involved a train, a platform, a passenger, and an observer on the platform. That exercise ultimately resulted in Einstein developing a question that became the basis for his Special Theory of Relativity.   His simple notion of a "thought experiment" helped me develop the skill of explaining complex technical concepts and problems in a language that broader audiences can understand.

Mark Twain's influence has also had an enormous impact on my life. Twain's legendary insight and cutting wit on topics that span as wide as observations of human behavior to political movements are so densely recorded, they fill literal libraries. If you have ever been concerned that your manner of speaking or writing isn't "fancy" enough, I give you Mark Twain. His ability to deliver powerful prose in his distinct writing style with all the same affectations and accents of his spoken words proves you don't have to be fancy. You should just be yourself.

As anyone who has perused the historical record knows, those who found themselves the subjects of Mark Twain's sharper words often wished he would be anyone but himself. Time has dulled the memory of how powerful the words and potent the presence of Twain was in American society. It was akin to Einstein's weighty influence on the world.,. We see snapshots of these two men, white-haired, in their later years. But in their words and stories, I've found endless inspiration from every age and stage of their lives.

Mark Twain certainly had more influence during his lifetime and throughout history, but Will Rogers exhibited economic precision in language. He demonstrated mastery of what we now call a sound bite that very few people have ever achieved. I look up his quotes frequently as a reminder of how to communicate an enormous amount by saying very little. Long before television and the internet existed, Will Rogers figured out how to inspire others and to make them stop and think with the eloquence of brevity.

Discover (or rediscover) your muses to use them as a superpower in your speaking style and every other aspect of your content creation. Muses will help you hone your pitches and presentations as you develop your unique perspectives, stylings, and delivery.

Now, let's address those nagging fears.

Public speaking is a terrifying prospect for many people. As we've already discussed, you can be a speaker if you can hold a conversation. Perhaps you won't start as a great or even a good speaker; those levels only come with practice for most of us.

But you can defeat your fears or anxieties about public speaking by drawing from your confidence in daily conversations. Simply ordering a meal, discussing the day's events with your child, and sharing information with your colleagues are inherent forms of public speaking. When I am asked how I've defeated my fears and anxieties when I get up on a stage in front of hundreds or thousands of people, I have two pieces of advice to offer.

First, embrace the fear!

I know. You are sure that somewhere in this book, I said I didn't fear public speaking! You're thinking, "Aha! I've caught him!"

However, I never said I wasn't afraid of speaking. I have just said that fear isn't an acceptable rationalization that should keep you from speaking. I fight my fears and anxieties every time I speak. The trick is understanding what exactly makes you scared to stand up and share your thoughts. I have a few ideas about what you might be afraid of because they are the universal fears most people experience when speaking publicly. These are the things that I'm afraid of, too.

Failure, embarrassment, and criticism comprise the universal trinity of public speaking fears.

These fears sound basic, common, and obvious. In truth, they fit each of these descriptors. However, how our fears manifest is very personal. The manifestation of our fears is just as unique as our fingerprints. When I manage my fear of failure, I'm not concerned about falling off the stage, throwing up, or forgetting my lines. My fear of failure is rooted in my obsession with wanting to impart some small amount of value to my audience or listeners. I don't want to waste people's time. I hope to offer something valuable to my audience each time I speak. I don't have unreasonable expectations when I speak. I don't believe I will change anyone's life or facilitate an epiphany that changes an entire industry. I want to make a small difference every time I speak.

Because I understand the root of my fear, I know how to manage and mitigate it. When I speak in front of any sized crowd, I frequently open my presentation by saying, "My goal is to make sure you leave today's session with just one new nugget of knowledge or one new way to look at the problem or challenge you are facing." By laying out my expectations at the beginning of a presentation, I'm reminding myself what needs to be done. I'm also creating a scoreboard to keep that fear of failure in check.

At the end of the presentation, I'll ask, "Today, if something that I shared has inspired you, motivated you, or changed your mind about something, raise your hand." This simple tactic confirms that my fear was unnecessary and that I made a positive impact, even in a small way. It also serves as an important point of feedback. We will get to the importance of feedback after we cover how to conquer fear.

Embarrassment is also a constant companion for me when I'm speaking. Or rather, the fear of being embarrassed is an ever-present shadow. You must do a lot of head-checking with yourself when you are an extemporaneous speaker like me. A slip of the tongue or an unfortunate choice of words could embarrass me and unintentionally offend any people in my audience. Sure, there are fears of embarrassment, including ripping my pants onstage or failing to see the ketchup stain on my shirt before I speak. These are not the improbable nuisances I spend my energy worrying about. My words accidentally causing hurt or harm to someone I don't know is a paralyzing fear. This is the place from which my fear of embarrassment stems.

For speakers who are persistent in their preparation and those who use notes and memorize their scripts, fear of using the wrong words or analogies might never be a problem. Speaking off-the-cuff allows folks like me to be "in the moment," but it comes with the risk of dropping the ball. The trick I use to mitigate the risks of tripping over my tongue is always keeping my audience in view. I remind myself constantly that I am talking to human beings. While this sounds incredibly simplistic, it is very easy to stop seeing your audience when you are speaking. Not seeing the people in front of you is a real thing, whether it is a small group or a large conference hall. I don't know if there is a scientific name for this phenomenon, but you can truly stop seeing the people before you in the thick of a presentation.

When you dehumanize the environment around you, it becomes way too easy to speak glibly or cavalierly. Not seeing who you are talking to leads to a higher probability of letting something fly from your mouth directly to your audience without engaging your brain. After covering my last big fear, criticism, I'll return to how to "see" your audience. It is an incredibly powerful trick to successfully engage with and impact your audience as a public speaker.

Many people fear criticism, which can be paralyzing. Our ideas are our babies, and nobody likes to have their baby called ugly. Hearing someone hack away at what we've spent time and effort creating and sharing is painful. That pain is the root of the paralyzing fear of criticism.

At the beginning of this book, I shared my story of being called a charlatan for sharing a very informed opinion about election security. That criticism had me waving my figurative hands wildly and trying to tell my critics, *"No, you don't know my experience and background in this space. I'm not a fraud."* I've since learned not to take this type of criticism personally. This is a challenging fear to overcome until we build an internal ability to process and manage criticism by pushing it into the "not personal" bucket.

Our fear of criticism is one problem to sort through, but our response to criticism also demands our awareness. Criticism doesn't just tear us down. It can catalyze unhealthy responses and exchanges with our followers and our critics. As innovators, experienced practitioners, or highly knowledgeable people in our fields of effort, we can quickly become overzealous believers in our opinions. Sometimes, we can convince ourselves that our opinions are not only truths but THE truth. Criticism of what we believe to be a singular truth only we know is perceived as a personal attack. When this happens, criticism triggers anger, bloviation (one of my favorite words of all time), and even rage. When our unguarded response to criticism drives this behavior, the world around us can and will quickly revoke that "expert" title they granted us.

Learning to control our fear of criticism can mitigate the possibility of being intellectually beaten down by the people who entrusted us to teach them. A thoughtful response (rather than a fear-fueled reaction) to criticism can eliminate an emotionally volcanic eruption that could end our pursuit of sharing our knowledge with our communities of practice. The method I use to conquer my fear of criticism isn't the only one, but I've found it to be very effective in my area of focus.

I invite my critics to join me.

Join? Like, come up on stage or take a seat with the panel I'm on?

No. I ask everyone in the audience to participate in the discussion I'm hosting. Very frequently, when I'm speaking, and usually within the first couple of minutes of a presentation I'm giving, I share something very specific with the audience.

"I've shared my background and experiences with you. But I want you to know I am not an expert. I'm someone who has accumulated a lot of bruises, scars, and broken bones, learning and growing in this field. I can probably tell you more things you shouldn't do based on my mistakes than what you should do. Some things I will share with you might be contentious or challenging, or you might disagree with me completely. But this is a dialogue, and there isn't enough debate in our line of work. So please don't hesitate to come up afterward to share your thoughts with me."

This approach is powerful. I know because I've had many people come up to me after a presentation. They do not approach me to debate or argue but to tell me that they've never heard a speaker in technology actively offer themselves up for that kind of feedback. I have also had several people approach me after speaking and say, "I agreed with most of what you said, but I think you were wrong on this point." Inviting the people I'm speaking to into an extended conversation defuses the less desirable behaviors of the critic and myself. I've laid the ground rules for engagement, extended an invitation to criticize me, and made my audience an active part of my presentation.

We've all grown up hearing that constructive criticism is helpful. In our personal and professional lives, going back to our school-aged days, we are encouraged to seek out constructive criticism. Asking to be criticized, constructively or otherwise, feels like we are exposing ourselves and making ourselves vulnerable, so we struggle to pursue criticism. For a public speaker, adopting an invitation tactic like the one I use is one way to actively ask for an audience to provide quality control of your message, your methods, and your delivery. I like to think that while anyone who comes to hear me speak is interested in my frequency, their input is the ingredient I need to fine-tune constantly. And I learn so much from the input that I receive from audiences. Whether it is a suggestion to research a historical event that I haven't considered or to follow another thought leader in my space that I wasn't aware of, these little nuggets of wisdom help me build and grow my skills and knowledge.

By being direct enough to say I'm no expert, that my goal is and always will be constantly learning, and then sharing that knowledge with others, I effectively pull the teeth out of the tiger's mouth. I'm not afraid of criticism anymore. I seek it out in a way that is healthy for everyone. One of the problems we face in many professions is a lack of reasonable, data-informed, and healthy debate. Our professional worlds can become an echo chamber where experts and leaders simply parrot the industry's talking points. Being open to criticism instead of avoiding it is a way to eliminate the echo.

Inviting my critics to join me and my listeners to engage with me led to another important discovery about public speaking.

One of the absolute worst pieces of advice I've ever heard about public speaking is, "Picture your audience in their underwear." First, in today's day and age, this seems like a surefire path to a guaranteed HR violation. Second, it is a terrible piece of advice. Why would your audience, in their underwear, be any less frightening than if they were all wearing giant down-filled parkas? What your audience is wearing is meaningless.

Most of the advice I've heard about public speaking from people who are just casual speakers or presenters is just as bad. "Find a spot on the wall above your audience's head and speak to that." What? If it's a decent-sized crowd in a conference hall, you'll probably look directly into a spotlight and burn your retinas out of your eyeballs. If it is a small crowd, you'll look like you hit yourself in the forehead with a hammer and gone loopy.

Trying to actively ignore your audience or imagine them as something they are not will not improve your public speaking one iota. Pretending they aren't there can lead to malapropisms or embarrassing comments, as I have already discussed. Don't dehumanize your audience with any of these poorly advised tricks. Embrace the human attendees to your presentation by not giving a presentation.

This leads to the second piece of advice I have to offer about public speaking.

Have a conversation with one person in the room and let everyone else listen in.

This isn't the standard advice given of "pick someone in the room and focus on them." It is a bit more abstract than that. Isolating your focus on one single person in a crowd can result in disaster. You don't want to end up pacing back and forth on a speaker stage, never taking your uncomfortable gaze off that poor, unfortunate soul you decided to stare at for 30 minutes.

Your delivery will be awkward and inauthentic, even if your message is dynamic, informative, and inspiring. There is no faster way to lose an audience than by making them uncomfortable. Just like when you are at a concert and go home saying, "I swear, Taylor Swift was looking right at me!" Your audience members can go home and say, "So, this guy was so creepy. He was giving his presentation and staring at me the whole time."

What I do is regularly change the one person I'm talking to. I start with the woman in the 3rd row on the right with the jacket on, and then 3 minutes later, I move to the man in the back row left with the ball cap. Then, I move on to the middle, where a guy with his head down is looking at his phone, followed by the woman on the far left in the fifth row who is nodding and taking notes. Sometimes, I even let people in on this secret when presenting. I'll let the audience know that I'm having a conversation and want them to listen in on it. This is a good reinforcement technique, so I don't forget to use this approach in my speaking engagements.

I usually do it when giving a presentation over 45 minutes long. Longer-format speaking gigs can be great for extemporaneous speakers like me because we can get all our stories in. Still, they can lead to wandering aimlessly around our core material if we don't focus. Focusing our energies on a conversation with individuals in the audience helps reduce that wandering problem.

The other benefit of conversing with one person at a time and letting everyone else listen in is that it opens your senses to gathering feedback while speaking. The ability to gather feedback while you are in the middle of your presentation is something that you develop with practice. I don't know that I've ever met anyone born with the natural ability to sense feedback. It takes practice speaking repeatedly and reaching a comfort level that opens your sensory channels. Once you've spoken several times, you'll begin to function in a different mode, where you can feel how your audience responds and engages. Not just as a group, but you'll also pick up individual signals from your audience members.

Feedback is a vital road sign for public speakers. We tune what we say and do based on feedback. Much like a stand-up comic says, "That joke slayed, I could feel it," public speakers can reach a level where audience response is palpable. Feedback is a bit addicting. Once you are feeling and hearing the laughs, the coughs, the uncomfortable moving in chairs, the claps, or the lonely sound of a dog howling in the distance with fluency, you will most likely begin to ask and seek feedback from your audience actively. These signals are how you can effectively measure that connection we should strive for as speakers. "Engaging" your audience is a common bit of advice, but what exactly does it mean? It means seeking out and asking for your audience's participation and then registering their feedback.

In the previous chapter, I discussed the complexities of connecting with your audience. It isn't just connecting with a single emotion.   It is about connecting with your audience and their collective feedback across a spectrum of different emotions, memories, and feelings. I shared the school board story as an example of how to reach a place within the hearts and minds of your audience that spurred them to think differently about the problem. While that story was powerful, it was a comparative analogy. I asked the audience to take a thought experiment trip with me that involved triggering their emotions about their community, their children, and their feelings about safety and security and then applying them to a digital equivalent. It wasn't a perfect equivalent. A bad guy breaking into your data isn't the same as a bad guy in the middle of your 3rd grader's school building. However, it was a relevant way to transfer emotion from an understood physical experience in the real world to a comparable digital event.

You need to find stories with explicit meaning and relevance in your community. While analogies and metaphors are incredibly helpful and effective tools for any speaker, this emotional abstraction is sometimes less effective than specific examples from our profession-al experiences. The world's premier lifeguard telling stories about airplane safety is probably not the best way to engage their audience. Relevance demands that you approach some topics with events and observations that your audience understands within the context of their professional life.

When I leverage these topics in my speaking engagements, they become my most emotional presentations. In my personal mission to make the digital world a safer place for everyone, the stories I bring to my community sound more like a fiery Sunday morning sermon. When I speak to people in my professional community, I feel like I'm talking to the front-line troops who can fix the problems plaguing the digital world. Yet, even with a hall filled with fellow cybersecurity warriors, connecting and getting the message across can be a challenge.

Storytelling, which leverages abstraction like the school example I used, may not move the needle with a group that has come through the same career path or has the same community interests as you have. Specification, or taking your story in the direction of concrete facts instead of emotional themes, and finding a storyline that drives to incontrovertible points is the way. It will also yield emotional re-sponses, but what we want to achieve with a group of our peers and colleagues is action. I'll share an example highlighting the difference between abstraction and specification in storytelling.

In my role in the digital identity field, one of the biggest challenges has been making progress and improvement against the bad guys. You see the news daily, so I won't belabor the point that the losses and damage created by those bad guys are getting worse constantly. This begs the question: if companies are fully aware that the world of digital security is worsening, why aren't they moving as fast as possible to improve it? Great question! In my industry and within my community, even the clear evidence that the bad guys are winning doesn't seem to be enough to motivate the people who are best equipped and trained to fight the bad guys, which is frustrating since my community is cybersecurity. We are the protectors and the defenders in that digital world.

This is a clear disconnect, or cognitive dissonance, between emotions and actions in my field. Even many of us in technology treat the digital world as separate from our everyday lives. Because we have created this detachment between our real and digital lives, we lack the same perceptions of the damages and pain caused in that digital world. It is the same as someone punching us in the face or keying scratches onto our cars. Those types of physical aggression make us fuming mad. But someone threatening us online registers as something trivial. For a story to have meaning and relevance for this audience, it requires exposing the truth that the damage and pain caused in the digital world is real and that it manifests all around us every day.

The digital world provides pathways to damage and harm in the real world. Whether it is financial loss, fraud, bullying, trafficking, or blackmail, the internet world has provided a platform for a lot of bad things. Making things worse is the lack of holistic investigative reporting on the scale or extent of the harm that hackers cause in society. Cybersecurity-related studies are almost always oriented to the security industry and all of us techno-geeks who work in it. Those studies focus on how attacks are executed, not on the damage that results from those attacks on the average person.

Thankfully, I'm friends with Eva Casey-Velasquez, the President and CEO of the Identity Theft Resource Center. Her organization serves as a scorekeeper of only a small percentage of the damages inflicted upon people. The Identity Theft Resource Center documents case samples of people who have had their personal digital information stolen and used by the bad guys to open credit lines, steal money, and destroy people's finances and reputations. The organization publishes regular reports on this problem and maintains a website that provides mountains of data about it.

Every time a new headline story about another company getting hacked breaks, it usually comes with the following statement: "We are happy to report that no credit card or banking information was stolen." But what the public relations and crisis management departments of those companies don't tell you in those well-crafted media releases is – the bad guys stole everything else about you. They may not have gotten your credit card or banking information, but they got their hands on plenty of your personal data. Your address, active cell phone number, entire transaction history with that company, and your relationship with any number of products in their catalog are exposed. The bad guys now know how long you've lived at your address, how many times you've refinanced your house and the makes, models, and years of your vehicles. These core details about your life are the only precious things that the company you trusted with your data has given up to data thieves. But at least they didn't give away your checking account number, right?

This data, which the bad guys have repeatedly stolen, allows those same bad guys to build a digital copy of you. Then, they used that digital copy of you to do awful things in your name. Those awful things include stealing money, cheating companies, opening accounts, collecting money, funding terrorist organizations, sustaining organized crime, and supporting human trafficking. Your stolen and copied digital identity is the economic engine that drives many terrible things in the real world.

Doesn't it relieve you that the bad guys didn't get your credit card info and banking data?

Every time a company you do business with is breached, the message in those media statements is, "Good news. We didn't let them steal your financial information, but we let them steal everything else about you."

You would think that this set of circumstances and consequences would be enough to motivate an entire global army of cybersecurity professionals to spring into action. Most security practitioners are overwhelmed by exhaustion, frustrated by corporate politics, starved for meaningful funding, or so cynical that they believe things will never get better in the war against the bad guys. This isn't a criticism of my fellow security colleagues; it is a hard truth about what we face daily when defending our companies, organizations, and agencies.

So, what kind of story and specificity would motivate this audience to action? Eva Casey-Velazquez has years of data, evidence, and case studies to draw from as a starting point. During my many interactions with Eva as a podcast guest and fellow panelist, she shared a story with me that has become a core narrative I use with technical audiences in my field of work. It goes like this.

"I worry sometimes that those of us who work in security are so buried in the challenges of the job and our corporate dysfunction. It becomes hard for us to draw a connection between our work and the positive benefits that it yields for the average person. The benefits it provides our family, friends, and neighbors are difficult to define. We've become so separated from the consequences of bad digital security and catastrophic breaches that we lose sight of the fact that what we do every day matters. What we do every day depends on us getting security right.

One of the things that I get most frustrated about within our community is the lack of emotional connection to this job. More than a few people are sitting in the audience who firmly believe that the damage and harm created in the digital world isn't that big of a deal. They think that nobody is getting hurt. Banks are making people whole when their accounts get ripped off. Grandmothers and grandfathers who suffer social engineering attacks that clear out their retirement and life savings are not that big an issue. They've got a family that can help them out. Nobody dies because their data got hacked. Right?

I wish that were true. I wish the digital world were some mystical and magical place entirely separate from our day-to-day lives. The truth is much harsher than that. People have been killed by hackers and social engineers engaged in swatting and shutting down hospital network equipment in emergency rooms and surgical suites. The bad guys pay no heed to the physical damage they cause. Except for a small category of bad actors who are like Michael Caine's description of the Joker in Dark Knight, 'Some men just want to watch the world burn.'"

In my work with Eva Casey-Velasquez at the Identity Theft Resource Center, Eva shared a story that proves our tone-deaf attitude to the damages caused by the bad guys who have repeatedly stolen our personal data. Her story shared the impact of bad guys who have stolen our personal data from companies that refused to be good stewards of our information. Companies always publish a media statement that says the attack they suffered was "sophisticated" and no credit card data or banking information was stolen. Rarely are these data thefts "sophisticated," and the bad guys keep stealing our personal data because it is valuable.

Let me tell you about the young lady who was the first in her family to get accepted to college. When it came time to register and place deposits for tuition and seek financial aid, this young lady and her family made a terrible discovery. Her personal data had been stolen before she even entered her teenage years. Which breach was her data stolen in? No one knows for sure. Kids video and online games, medical information entrusted to a doctor's office or insurance company, or information stolen from a school district server where security isn't a well-funded initiative within the technology department are all possibilities. The data could have come from any of these sources or an entirely different one. Or the data could have been sourced from all of them, which the bad guys then used to create a fictitious person, a synthetic identity.

So, this young lady and her family spent the next three years fighting to clear her credit record. It is important to take a moment to share an incredibly painful truth about what this family endured. Not only did the companies and organizations they entrusted their business to fail to protect their data, but the system forced this family and every other victim of data theft to clean up and rectify the damages they suffered as a victim. Personal data theft and its damages are the only crimes victims are forced to fix on their own.

I know it hurts to hear this. But that's our fault.

And the damages that this young lady suffered are real. This isn't some white-collar 'victimless' crime. For three years, she couldn't begin college at all. She lost three years of attending school with her cohort. She lost three professional earning years. That alone could be worth several hundreds of thousands of dollars. She is three years behind on professional career growth and promotions. She had to spend time, money, and personal labor to fix what others had broken for her and her family. Her life was put on hold because we, the security community, let her down and let her data get stolen multiple times.

Doesn't that make anyone mad here? Or are we embarrassed? Is this what we want our legacy to be? Children who are permanently damaged by the actions of bad guys because 'at least we didn't let them steal your credit card data, 11-year-old kid?' What about our elderly parents or grandparents?

If we must wait until we wake up as professionals to the reality that true and lasting damage to real-life human beings is happening every day because we aren't getting the job done in digital security, then things can only get worse from here.

This story I just told you isn't unique. It isn't an isolated incident or a limited sample that I cherry-picked to get your attention. The Identity Theft Resource Center tracks identity-related breaches every quarter of the year. The number of victims each quarter is in the tens of millions. The number of people they help with advice, guidance, and advocacy because their identities have been stolen using the data acquired in breach after breach is in the tens of thousands yearly.

What we need to ask ourselves is what we, as a community, are going to do about it. Isn't it time for us to be honest with ourselves and say that the way that we've been doing things for the last twenty years isn't working? Isn't it time for us to consider a different approach? The data sure seems to tell us that it is."

That is the story: a mini-case study of how a young lady had her life destroyed by a complacent and non-caring corporate world that demands all of her data but then refuses to protect it effectively. This story usually makes my audience very uncomfortable. There aren't shouts of approval, high-fives, and waving of hands. Nope. This story is embarrassing for us. This story is a mirror that forces us to realize that we do not, or choose not, to see the damaging consequences of breaches and exploits against our companies. We don't have the emotional attachment to get angry, disgusted, fed up, and motivated enough to make a difference.

A call to action isn't always a story wrapped in good feelings and a pretty ribbon. Sometimes, it will take sharing facts and evidence that figuratively punches the audience in the mouth. Being famous with 12 people gives us a margin for pushing boundaries and edges in these spaces. As I said, if you simply repeat your industry's same stories and standard lines, you won't get to FW12P. Everyone parroting the same thing, and all the heads nodding together in the conference hall does not lead to change, growth, or innovation.

If you've been honored by your peers and given the proverbial microphone, you are obligated to use it.

Using the influence you have been entrusted with by your peers for good and using these types of data-driven stories is how you pay back your community. You aren't onstage or recording that webinar or podcast so that you can put anyone down or shame them. No single person owns any or all the things that may be wrong or poorly prioritized in your field of expertise. You are a voice for the collective "we." As the old saying goes, always remember that when you point a finger at someone, you have four more fingers pointing back at you. Technically and biologically, you have three fingers pointing back at you and one thumb doing what thumbs do.

Storytelling is a powerful skill. It is a tool that helps people make an emotional connection with you, with each other, and with their career focus or personal interests and hobbies. By shifting your storytelling method from abstraction to specification, you can successfully move an audience with deeper technical or functional knowledge in a subject to emotional connection. For both kinds of storytelling, there is one more element that we need to consider.

Humility. (I told you it would come up again.)

The best micro-famous people I count as friends and colleagues all wear a mantle of humility. As this part of your career path is developed and grown, you will realize that the more you know and experience about a subject, the less you do know.   Diving deep into the waters of expertise does not result in an all-seeing, all-knowing expert. It creates a person who has consumed all the readily available knowledge about that thing, leaving them with unanswered questions and knowledge yet to be found or created.

The need to be humble may surprise people. If you have the kind of personality and motivation it takes to stand up in front of a bunch of people and shake their world with a new, unheard-of thinking on how to solve a problem, you probably aren't lacking in ego. Even if you might struggle initially with confidence, confidence has more to do with fear than it does with how big or small your ego is. Humility is hard for people with big egos.

Before I share my own experience and struggles with learning to be humble, this is a worthy moment to highlight one of many societal problems that shouldn't jeopardize or discourage so many people in this world. Men have the luxury of exhibiting both ego and humility with little consequence. While some may disagree, the evidence supports this conclusion. There are substantially more recognized experts and micro-famous people who are male than there are females. In almost every profession and avocation, whether on conference stages or as panel members, the most common constant is men. And in many nations, men who do not come from the diverse backgrounds of their broader populations. Whether we are arrogant or self-effacing, men get a wider margin of tolerance for our behaviors and demeanors than others.

While I clearly cannot speak from a woman's perspective or from the perspective of many cultures who don't have the advantages of others in society, I know what I see and have enjoyed the benefits of being an invited participant in many different cultures. For those not in the unfairly favored class, a display of ego can be treated like a show of unearned entitlement. For women, it leads to labels and epithets that males rarely must endure. Displaying humility, the most expert of experts in the world can and sadly are all too often judged as weak if they are women.

It should go without saying that this inequity and inequality in treatment and hurdle to success just shouldn't exist. While finishing this book, I attended an enormous security conference where the speaking population represented some of the deepest experts available in the world of digital security. As I write this, a considerable number of the attendees to that conference are in an uproar about a security company that adorned their events with female models in revealing attire and had lampshades on their heads.

Another security company distributed pink fuzzy handcuffs to visitors to their booth. Handcuffs, by themselves, really aren't worth getting bothered over at a cybersecurity conference. Lockpicking is a very popular event at security conferences. It was reports of many comments and questions addressed to more than a few female attendees at the booth about the use of the ultimate handcuffs that made the situation inappropriate and awkward. This didn't happen 30 years ago; it happened in the summer of 2024.

What signals did this kind of objectification send to everyone in my industry? What message did it convey to the thousands of exceptional talents at this conference who were women? For many professionals at this conference, whatever the intended message was, the poorly handled delivery generated a lot of anger and disgust.

Another benefit of being famous with 12 people is how many incredible experts from every walk of life, culture, background, upbringing, and gender I spend time with and share events and stages with. My colleague Eve Maler is most definitely one of those amazing experts. When we first met, I had no idea what her work and advocacy had meant in the context of technology's history. She never mentioned it. I never researched her background. I just enjoyed a wonderful set of conversations. I established a professional relationship with her, and we have been interacting with each other at conferences and industry groups for several years now.

In a casual conversation with another great friend and expert, John Kindervag, John shared a story about how Eve attended a keynote presentation by a male senior executive. When the exec asked whether anyone in the audience had experience with the technology protocol he was speaking about, Eve raised her hand. When it was clear that the speaker got several points about that protocol wrong during the exchange, John told me that he told the event organizer to encourage that male executive to stop speaking.

When asked why, John simply said, "She co-invented the protocol he's trying to explain to her."

In a world where too many knuckleheads are inclined to dismiss Eve's knowledge and contributions as an expert, Eve stands above it. Her capacity to do so shouldn't be a thing. It shouldn't be a muscle or a reflex that anyone must develop.   I firmly believe that learning how to check your ego is a powerful contributor to increasing the appeal of your brand. Eve is one of the best embodiments of this trait

I've ever known. But her story also shows the frustrating complexities and societal challenges that too many voices still need to endure.

I will be transparent. Humility was challenging at the beginning of my journey to being famous with 12 people.

I'm not a Type A personality or hyper-competitive by nature. Any number of tests and assessments I took in the corporate world confirmed those facts, but they also showed that I like to be recognized for my work. Further, they revealed that I hold very strong, some might say very stubborn, beliefs in my observations and opinions. My personality skews toward always wanting to be right, never wanting to be wrong, and enjoying a bit of acknowledgment now and then.

Let's be intellectually honest about these specific traits. Those characteristics are nothing more than manifestations of my pride. When you reach a point where your professional brand earns you a title like "expert," it is easy to stop being humble and become egotistical and boastful. You know precisely the types of people I'm speaking about. They can only frame their stories, guidance, reminisces, and teachings by saying "I" about 297 times.

"I invented this."

"I ran the world's largest that."

"I conquered the unconquerable thing."

"I" is the fingerprint of the ego, and it creates a problem for those who listen to and follow you. They aren't a part of what you are doing. They are relegated to the role of observer. Maybe even the role of a distant observer. "I" completely invalidates the relationship you are trying to build with a very large "everyone." You are both a spokesperson for and a member of the community you are a part of as a speaker. You aren't the captain or admiral; you are not your community's president or prime minister. You are a part of your community. And "I" is the great community killer.

Some people show up at the start of this micro-famous road trip with giant and uncontrolled egos. Some people believe in their own advertising before getting their first speaking platform or media quote. Don't worry. The same rules apply to them. Either they learn to embrace and exercise humility, or their star will only rise so far and rapidly fade. Why?

Nobody likes someone who is an asshole.

They like assholes even less when they are also know-it-alls.

I have two recommendations on how to pursue humility actively.

First, always be hungry, starving even, for knowledge.

Second, always be comfortable asking yourself an important question, "What if everything I believe is wrong?"

By combining the self-actualization needed to be constantly trying to learn more and the self-awareness required to doubt the validity of your theories and observations, you create a powerful recipe for humble pie.

I was on a trip where I spoke in several European countries. When I walked into one of the conferences in Munich, I ran into an old friend and colleague, Andrew Hindle, in the registration line. Andi and I hadn't seen each other in person for quite some time, so we went straight into the "how are things going" talk track.

I told Andi that the last half-year of my working career, leading up to the moment we were catching up, had made me think that everything I knew about identity and cybersecurity was utterly wrong. This surprised Andi, and we began to unpack why I felt that way.

The reason was as simple as this: By focusing so much time and energy on research, reading, and speaking, I had come to feel that the very foundation of our discipline was no longer relevant to protecting the digital world. The digital world has changed so fundamentally that people our age are applying our 30-year-old experiences, methodologies, and terminologies, which has kept us from success.

Andi encouraged me to explore my doubts, not wallow in them. The conversation led to me submitting several speaking proposals focused on the gaps and disconnects I felt were contributing to the problem. It was productive for me to bare my soul to Andi that I had serious concerns about what I thought I knew. Thankfully, someone highly regarded as an expert in the same field was more than just a listening ear. He helped me to identify a whole new set of ideas to consider.

Are you ready to walk up to someone in your area of focus and say, "Hey, is it possible that I don't know what the hell I'm doing," and receive their feedback? Being in love with our own opinions can lead to our downfall. Our ego can be our enemy if we don't exercise this kind of introspection regularly. Doing so will help us stay relevant to our audience, especially when speaking to them.

Going back to Socrates, many great thinkers and philosophers have made it clear that knowledge is being aware of our ignorance. If that isn't a statement that will keep you humble, I don't know of a better one. Mark Twain may have gotten close with, "My father was an amazing man. The older I got, the smarter he got."

As an expert, you are not a singularity. As we've already discussed, experts, expertise, innovation, and paradigm-breaking thinking can come from anywhere. If anyone can be an expert, you can just as quickly stop being one. All these factors and more should help you to keep from getting a fat head and disrespecting or insulting your audience.

Humility will come up several more times in this book. It doesn't just apply to speaking. It also applies to writing, networking, collaborating, and brand-building. These universal truths apply in every possible area of personal and professional life, in every industry, and in every niche of skill, talent, and expertise.

You are not a solo act.

Life is a team sport.

You are on stage and out front because of your audience, not because of you.

Becoming a speaker worth hearing will serve you well across every engagement, discussion, and interaction related to your area of focus. Being a different kind of speaker in tone, temperament, storytelling, and connection will create more opportunities to speak. When you combine this ability with your personal branding, you've blended the perfect cocktail to increase your visibility within your community and grow your career toward becoming a recognized voice.

You're on your way to being famous with 12 people.

BRAND YOU

Do I need a personal brand, a professional brand, or both? And where do I even start when it comes to building one? In this chapter, we'll break down the essentials of branding, explore the differences between personal and professional brands, and guide you through creating a brand that truly represents you.

Quick survey. How many new people did you meet, follow, or listen to last year in your career, volunteer work, or avocation?

People you networked with, people you met at conferences, the bar, and those you have heard on a podcast or watched on some media channel all count. Take the estimated number and ask yourself the following questions. How many of them do you remember by name? How many did you make the effort to connect with or follow online? If the answer for you is only one or two folks, why?

We often think of a personal brand only in reference to other people. They have a brand, not me. Many think of personal brands only applying to influencers or media personalities.

Personal brands aren't for regular people, right? Before I answer that question with an entire chapter on Brand You, think about those couple of people you met last year that you stay connected with or still follow.   Then, come back to that question of why.

If your answer to that question is because of their personality, how they present themselves, or how they focus on you and the things that interest or motivate you, then you've already begun to assemble the pieces of their personal brand. It is about more than just having a dazzling personality.

You've met many interesting people with great personalities but aren't staying connected with or following them. Their personal brand is built on the combination of who they are, what they know, how they present it, and "what's in it for you."

Yep. Anyone can have a personal brand.

If you disagree, I offer this question. Do you know of anyone in the wide, wide world who has a personal brand that you believe shouldn't? Again, why? It is probably because none of the pieces I mentioned above sit well with you. They don't have any relevance for you, so you are probably prone to discount their need for a personal brand. You don't like what they represent, whether it is their ideas, opinions, or approach. Even if they have outstanding personalities, you'd still believe they shouldn't have a personal brand. At your most congenial, you'd simply tell people, "They aren't my cup of tea." This means a personal brand isn't just your personality in isolation. You must intentionally develop a personal brand.

Personal branding takes time, effort, planning, and thoughtfulness. It is also important to remember that a personal brand isn't the only thing you have to put effort into when trying to be famous with 12 people. One thing that most of us who gain any recognition in our communities of practice have in common is that we have day jobs. There are exceptions to this rule. Many personalities and experts have reached the field of freedom known as retirement. A select few earn enough income from their expertise-related activities that they don't have to hold a position in a company. I know a lot of micro-famous people. I can tell you that in the sample population I interact with, very few have achieved either condition. We have day jobs, possibly with a professional brand, and we have personal brands.

Almost all of us must manage the juggling act of managing dual brands. This chapter will discuss this quite a bit, focusing on building a personal brand while navigating the synergies and disconnects between it and your professional brand. Part of my journey in building a personal brand was meeting the challenge of figuring out this dual-branding dynamic.

It might sound complicated and intimidating to manage a pair of brands, let alone one. Thankfully, three common ingredients link personal and professional brands. They are both branding types' philosophical and functional foundations and apply to any successful brand.

Confidence, consistency, and authenticity.

Confidence and consistency will get a lot of attention in this chapter, as well as how to build a personal brand in general. Authenticity will get a moment all its own in the next chapter.

I didn't intentionally create my brand to pursue a nebulous "expert" title.   I also knew nothing about this dual-branded thing. Shortly after establishing my personal brand, one of my most influential mentors and leaders encouraged me to amplify and accelerate its development. I thought his proposal was crazy. But Andre Durand insisted, and he was right. Learning how to craft a unique personal brand started well before I met Andre, so we'll get to that part of the story further in this chapter. We need to rewind to the year I departed from the corporate fold, in 2016.

I thought I was stepping away from the corporate world for a year to re-group before finding my next Chief Information Security Officer role. I was burned out from decades of hard work and unkept promises. The real hallmark of my professional career wasn't technology operations or cybersecurity. No, I was a "fixer". The problem with being a fixer in American business is you are always told there is a pot of gold at the end of the broken rainbow that you fix and put back on track.

Once you fix the problem, you almost always find out that there was never a pot of gold, and the promises offered to you were hollow and meaningless. All too often, the pot of gold isn't there, but another bucket of crap to clean up is always waiting.

Don't misunderstand me; I wouldn't trade my corporate experiences for anything. They made me who I was when I reached the end of my patience and persistence, leading me to realize that I needed to try something new. I left the company offices behind and went to work as a strategic advisor in security solutions. I took my experience as a corporate C-level executive and used it to counsel and help other C-level executives.

Something unexpected happened during my supposed break between corporate jobs.

I started my advisory role with a company I had been a customer of for several years, working with the sales team. I had a great time. I would meet with senior leaders at companies to discuss the latest cybersecurity trends and concerns. It was a fun job, full of dinners, conferences, and meaningful discussions on improving things.

Within this company, there was a consulting practice that focused on identity security. The leaders in the consulting group found out that I had previously led the identity and security functions at a couple of companies. Would I consider doing some speaking engagements and moderated panels on the subject?

Remember what I said earlier about the corporate world and inability to speak? Yeah, that was me for more than 20 years. I hadn't done any professional speaking until that moment in my career. I had no interest in returning to doing functional work in the identity space, but what's the harm in talking about it, right? Talking about it sounded easy enough.

Even though I had no experience getting up in front of dozens or hundreds of people to talk about security things, I did what I've always done. Throughout my career, when offered an opportunity to do something slightly beyond my experience, I simply said "yes." I've always told people I'm unsure if I say yes because I'm smart and know what rewards are ahead or because I'm dumb and have no idea what I'm getting myself into. Whichever of these two dynamics drives my urge to raise my hand and take on crazy projects, the strategy has worked more times than it has failed.

The first few speaking engagements weren't difficult. I knew the topic and felt confident in that knowledge. In no way, shape, or form was I an expert. I was just someone sharing their experiences with a group of people who were interested in that same topic. I don't remember anything remarkable or revelatory from those first few times stepping up on a stage or a podium, but it laid the groundwork for what would come next.

When I started speaking in public, I brought a couple of unique characteristics—not a personal brand, per se, but idiosyncrasies and personality quirks. Some go back to a time long before I was in a professional career.

Because of a life-long interest in fashion (shout out to Mom and Pops for the GQ subscription birthday gift when I was 12), I was showing up to my first speaking gigs in an outfit I had gotten comfortable wearing every day. For several years in the banking industry, I had adopted the habit of wearing a bowtie. All the credit for that accessory goes to a mentee, former employee, and dear friend, Tony Fluellen. One day, during a regular one-on-one meeting at the bank we worked at together, Tony said, "You're always wearing a blazer, Richard; you should wear a bowtie, too."

That's it. There isn't anything more complicated about my wearing a bowtie than a young staff member suggesting it one day.

Since it had been my style in the corporate world, I just carried it over to my new role. Little did I know that it would become something associated with my brand. After my first few speaking sessions, somebody said, "Hey, I've been really looking forward to hearing from the guy with the bowtie." That label stuck.

Shortly after the bowtie became a fixture, there were cocktails. A Manhattan cocktail in my hand, to be precise.

Many of the speaking sessions I was doing were either lunch-hour or dinner-hour keynotes, leading to a panel discussion with people from other companies in my solution area. I like cocktails. It was dinner time. I enjoy cocktails with my dinner. I ordered one at an event and held it while giving the presentation. And boom! It's the guy who does cybersecurity talks while drinking a cocktail.

Without planning or deep thoughts on my brand, I showed up with a bowtie and a cocktail at a speaking event.

It was fun, funny, and a little quirky. Before I could blink, these characteristics became hallmarks of my newly developing personal brand. The cocktail was also an example of how quickly and thoroughly your audience will ascribe something to you while you are trying to craft your brand.

After one event in New York, my very next speaking event, someone walked up to me and asked me why I didn't have a cocktail on stage. She had heard from a friend at the prior event that I'd have one in hand. At an event a couple of years later, the event coordinator informed me that one of her staff had a bartender waiting at the side stage to ensure I got a fresh Manhattan before walking up on stage.

In addition to these accidental accessories, I have a particular way of delivering presentations.

While this way of presenting comes naturally to me, many people who heard me perceived it as new and novel. This style is part of my personality, not some preconceived part of a personal branding plan.

I am an extemporaneous speaker.

I usually show pictures on the screen and tell a story about the image or the concept I'm trying to express with that visual. I don't do a script. I don't memorize line after line—not because I can't, but because it doesn't come across as genuine or authentic.

I know a lot of speakers who sound like every word coming out of their mouth has sprung forth from the mind like a fresh idea when they have memorized a very lengthy script word for word. I envy that level of command, both of language and self. It's awe-inspiring when you know it is happening. Not a single "um" or "uh," just precision of vision and speech in one tidy package. "Ums" and "uhs" aren't a problem and shouldn't deter you from speaking. Very few speakers have flawless, newscaster-quality speaking habits.

Many are like me. We labor over themes and ideas and then build an entire storyline around them but leave a healthy margin for spontaneity. We don't rehearse repeatedly to achieve perfection in our delivery. When you are speaking on stage, anything can happen. Events worth weaving into your narrative could have happened 2 hours before in the news cycle. I feel most comfortable focusing on an outline of items to cover instead of a script requiring memorization. This extemporaneous style is now a firmly embedded component of my personal brand.

I've also built a healthy reputation as someone who doesn't speak like a techie.

What does a techie speak like? Many of them dive deep into the details of their expertise, where only a few folks can keep up with them. A large percentage of them are, well, kind of dry. Many technical folks try to force a speaking style that is inconsistent with their personality, assuming it is how an audience expects them to present.

Some people think you must be funny to be listened to by an audience. I always tell people, "Don't try to be funny if you're not already at least dad-joke level funny." Trying to force funny into your speaking style, if you're not funny, will be sniffed out by your audience every time. Not every great speaker is funny, but you can't be dry like day-old toast. Sometimes, it is easier for technologists to hide behind data and technical terms rather than share some part of their personality with an audience.

TED Talks, to me, showcases the World Series All-Stars of public speaking. Watch a bunch of TED Talks in a row. Very few of them sound like stand-up comedy routines. The personalities of these speakers almost always shine through their material. Remember the memorized precision that sounds like the speaker is having a personal conversation with just you that I mentioned earlier? Those are TED Talks every time. These speakers aren't always funny, melodramatic, or overly serious. Still, their personalities are on full display.

TED Talk speakers add a crucial ingredient to their personalities: passion. Allow your personality to be free during your speaking engagements and focus on a topic you passionately believe in. You will be an entirely different presenter than almost everyone in your area of expertise. I found my personality and passion quickly when I first started speaking. Sometimes, it comes out funny; many times, it comes out serious. But it differs from almost anyone else who gets up on stage or in front of a microphone.

Those ingredients summed up my early speaking engagements: a bowtie, a cocktail, and a story delivered with personality and passion.

This brings us back to Andre Durand and his crazy proposal.

As a strategic advisor, I had been speaking publicly for a couple of years, which landed me an opening keynote presentation at a multi-day conference. Andre Durand was in the front row of the audience that morning. We had met a couple of times before that day and shared a few conversations, but none of those interactions prepared me for what happened next.

Andre took a picture of me on stage and texted it to the CEO of the company I was working for, saying, "Richard is a great speaker. I hope you are using his talents." The CEO responded, "LOL." A few weeks later, Andre called me.

He asked me to come to work for him.

After I got past the initial shock, we spent a few phone calls sorting out my role and responsibilities for the position he offered. The last discussion we had before the offer was finalized was when he made the proposal that I thought was crazy—the proposal that changed my life.

"I need you to have two brands. I need you to be "Richard Bird on behalf of Ping Identity," and I need you to be "Brand Richard Bird."

At first, I thought he was joking. Why would any company want me to join them and create or develop a personal brand alongside my company brand? I distinctly remember saying, "No, that's not possible. You can't have two personalities when you work for a company."

Andre was insistent, so I asked the obvious question. "Why?"

Andre told me that my role at Ping Identity would have a shelf-life. He explained that the company would change as we moved from a late-stage start-up to a publicly held company. He explained that it would change as the rest of our executive team would change over time. Things would change when I started to feel that I was losing touch with my operational experience or, worse, when the market no longer saw me as an operator but as just another player in a sales organization.

"And when that time here is done at Ping Identity, you will still have important things to say that need to be heard."

Andre laid that challenge down in front of me. A classic "put up or shut up" kind of moment. Either I believed I had something important to say about my professional passion, or I didn't. If I said I couldn't split myself into two distinct brands, I was fully admitting that what I had to share wasn't truly the passion I believed it to be. I could certainly still have been successful as a speaker on behalf of the company, but Andre was suggesting that there was something bigger to consider.

Andre saw it in me, even if I didn't see it in myself. He saw that I had this driving desire to fix the problems in this area of expertise. Somehow, he knew that I could figure out how to frame the message and stories in a way that would move an audience to action. He might have been betting on my potential rather than knowing that I would succeed, but he made me that offer.

It's not a spoiler to say I took the job. As it turned out, Andre was 100% accurate in his prediction that the job I took would have an expiration date.

What happened over my next three years working for Ping Identity were the learning experiences that became the foundation for this book. The other thing that happened was building a personal brand independent of but joined to a corporate brand. It not only changed the trajectory of my career, but it has helped me achieve at least a little bit of that "changing the world" momentum when it comes to my passion.

I don't believe Andre, or I are unique in discovering the power of a dual brand. Many start-ups seem to have grasped the value of an organic approach to amplifying their brands by encouraging the sharing of expertise by an evangelist, influencer, or personality. The community of personas like this in my field seems to grow daily. That growth isn't limited to technology or cybersecurity. These types of expert voices are growing in every field and industry.

Until recently, companies thoroughly discouraged building one's brand. Sometimes, it was even accompanied by overtures of termination or personnel actions. For companies that haven't embraced the value these kinds of roles can bring to their organization, discouraging personal branding may still be the case. The rare air of local, national, or international recognition has been reserved for the CEO and the CEO only.

Overall, the business world has figured out that while many genuine and sincere humans might be CEOs, many have a strategically curated brand that their company strictly manages. Those manufactured CEO personalities aren't authentic. I'm not saying that CEOs are inauthentic by design. I know many extraordinary, authentic CEOs and have been fortunate to work for a few. That said, the outward brand expression created for those business leaders can create an inauthentic feeling for the outside observer.

Authenticity is something the market craves, that we crave as individual human beings, and that followers and fans demand from those who are micro-famous. Remember, we are not talking about political leaders or social media influencers, but people who are famous with 12 people. The need for authenticity or displays of authenticity is up for debate when discussing politicians, celebrities, or TikTok phenoms. Macro-fame seems to allow for a large margin of fakery and inauthentic behavior. Why is this the case? I have no idea.

But authenticity is a critical currency for your career growth toward being micro-famous. If you feel authenticity isn't essential, ask yourself a question. How connected do you feel with any superstar CEO? Different question. How connected do you feel with the personality that you follow regularly in any given industry?

I bet that your answers to those two questions are very different.

A lot of CEOs are qualified experts. You can't just wing it while running a large corporate enterprise. If they aren't subject-matter experts, many are undoubtedly expert leaders. I'm going to guess that you don't feel any personal connection to these CEOs. Some of that may be attributed to the reality that you have no interest in being a CEO, so their brand doesn't represent anything inspiring to you. However, it is just as likely that you don't feel a connection because of that carefully crafted brand image that CEOs have built for them.

To a certain degree, a manufactured or processed professional brand is very understandable. A CEO has weighty obligations to manage. They are often the face of the company to the media, their broader industry community, and their customers. A personal brand that isn't consistent with the organization's message or introduces risk to the corporate brand has consequences for both the CEO and the company. A professional brand is virtually the only brand that a CEO can leverage. That doesn't mean there aren't a few high-profile CEOs with a personal brand.

One CEO comes to mind. Elon Musk. Elon is authentic in his personal brand, which shouldn't be confused with the idea that everyone digs his authenticity or his personal brand. However, he has a distinct and separate brand from his professional one. Arguably, his personal brand may have eclipsed his professional brand.

I'm confident that "play the Mario Brothers character Wario on Saturday Night Live" wasn't a request by one of Tesla's board members. Elon's personal brand has generated risk for Tesla, Twitter/X, and cryptocurrency exchanges. The difficulties of managing a dual brand when you are the leader of multiple companies probably can't be better highlighted by anyone other than Elon.

CEOs are stuck with a challenging balance act they cannot easily ignore. That balance is missing if their personal brand is out of alignment with their board, investors, and marketing executives' expectations for their professional brand. Elon Musk's imbalances resulted in a $20 million personal fine and another $20 million fine against Tesla, all because of his Twitter posts.

Influencing a stock's direction can be problematic for a CEO—like a go-to-jail problematic outcome if carried to the extreme. You can make that problem disappear by simply buying Twitter, but you and I don't have those resources available. If you do, please email me because I'd like to talk about coming to work for you.

The great news is that if you aren't a CEO, you have way more freedom to build that personal brand than they do. The CEOs might be getting all those big bonuses, but you, my friend, are free. You are free to build a personal and a professional brand in a responsible way that maximizes the effectiveness of both!

How do you build the dual-branded you, though?

The answer to that question is both mechanical and philosophical. Let's cover the philosophical components of confidence and consistency, first.

Here is an important rule to remember: No successful brands lack confidence. What kind of product would be successful if the company promoting it said, "We think it might work, but we're not sure?" What kind of brand would be successful if it trumpeted, "We're the fourth best solution you can buy!" If you are not confident in your positions, observations, ideas, and message, you must work on that first.

If you strive to be famous with 12 people, your personal and professional brands reflect your expertise and consistency. The quickest way to short-circuit your journey to being recognized as an expert is to be inconsistent. People worldwide demand and yearn for authenticity, as we've already discussed. Being inconsistent is just one hallmark of being inauthentic. People will feel that they can't trust you. And if they can't or won't trust you, "expert" is the last thing they'll call you.

Being consistent doesn't mean being inflexible or unteachable. It is easy to conflate consistency with immovability, but these aren't the same. Being flexible and teachable is a manifestation of your humility. Being consistent is about avoiding wild swings in your professional beliefs, passions, and focus. We become famous with 12 people most frequently due to our work in a defined problem domain. Sometimes, it is due to our work in a narrowly defined problem domain. If our audience believes that we change our opinions within those domains frequently, we aren't a true expert, or we won't be perceived as one.

Confidence and consistency don't mean you have to suffer the restriction of being too narrow in a subject matter expertise focus, though. As you build momentum during this part of your career growth, you'll be exposed to opportunities you may naturally explore as a speaker. My core area of focus has been digital identity. Yet my combination of personal and professional backgrounds and understanding of how identity knits everything together in the digital world has expanded my reputation. I naturally stretched into election security, nation-state hacking, government standards, and individual privacy.

Still, I must stay confident and consistent in my messaging and passion for digital identity to move into adjacent spaces and grow my brands.

Trust is the philosophical, existential, and metaphorical fuel for being famous with 12 people. If you are widely viewed as an expert in physical fitness, you can't suddenly change your entire perspective on the type of training style you have promoted as the most effective. Extolling the virtues of powerlifting for a few years, then waking up and telling the world, "I was wrong; yoga is the way," will have a massive dampening effect on the people who viewed you as a strength training guru.

It would be inconsistent to abruptly change your approach, philosophy, and thinking this way. Those who follow you will translate that inconsistency into a trust issue. I'll be the first to say that reaction might be unfair on their part. Maybe you did wake up one morning and realize your life calling was yoga after years of squatting 500 lbs. dissecting every possible tip, trick, and technique to accomplish that feat. It probably didn't happen that way, but it could have. This is where the challenge of managing a brand begins to become apparent.

Maybe a better example (for those who are old enough to remember) is the branding fiasco that Coca-Cola created for itself with the "old Coke versus New Coke" moment in history. The change in Coca-Cola's original formula has been called one of the biggest marketing catastrophes ever. We're talking about an event that was so devastating that even Coca-Cola tells the disaster story on its corporate website. There aren't many companies that highlight their biggest failures.

The drink was more than just a fizzy beverage for many Coca-Cola consumers. It was a mega-brand that, for decades, inspired people to buy not only curvy bottles filled with secret recipes but also memorabilia, clothing, and ephemera, with every variation of the Coca-Cola marketing slogan. The red and white Coca-Cola graphic isn't just instantly recognizable; it is instantly recognizable around the globe. You can stand in the middle of a market in Singapore, Dubai, or Nashville and immediately know where to get a Coke, regardless of the language you speak or understand. Coca-Cola conducted taste tests with over 200,000 people to select New Coke's flavor. You know what? None of that mattered at all. What mattered was consistency and trust.

In 1985, Coca-Cola announced the arrival of New Coke and immediately started receiving 5,000 complaint calls a day to their customer hotline. Within a few weeks, there were 8,000 complaint calls a day. Less than three months after the launch of New Coke, the company backtracked and declared that Coca-Cola would return using the original formula. Coca-Cola grossly underestimated their customers' loyalty and emotional attachment to their brand. The slightest inconsistency would have resulted in calls to their customer hotline. An enormous inconsistency, like throwing out the beloved original Coke flavor, nearly led their customers to a total revolt.

Your personal and professional brand is exactly like old Coke and new Coke.

You must credit Coca-Cola for figuring out how to put the toothpaste back in the tube when they re-introduced Coca-Cola Classic. Thirty-five years or more after the summer of discontent that Coke suffered in 1985, it is hard to argue with the fact that Coca-Cola learned its lessons from branding failures. They figured out how to capitalize on rebuilding trust through consistency and focus. By any metric you choose, Coca-Cola is 4 to 5 times larger a company than it was in 1985. They protected the growth and influence of the classic red-and-white brand and evolved and expanded through the nurturing of the additional brands they acquired.

Being consistent with your brand doesn't have to be a limiting factor. You can expand and evolve your personal brand. I highly encourage you to do so. You can also recover from fumbling on consistency like Coke did. However, failing to be consistent with your personal and professional brands can and will have consequences.

Let's say, for example, that your professional brand is built around the notion that you are a high-profile executive who shares tips on how to be successful. Let's also presume those tips include that you wake up at 4:30 a.m. every day, do an hour of exercise, and never drink a drop of alcohol. Your personal brand should not include photos posted on social media of you on a bender in some exotic tropical destination or seated at some resort restaurant with piled-up plates from the buffet in front of you.

There is nothing wrong with some heavy partying and eating excessively. However, if it is inconsistent with the brand you are promoting, you will create an inauthentic and untrustable "you." Your professional and personal brands will never stand a chance in the sunlight of our highly digitized world.

Mechanically, the work comes in maintaining this consistency and harmonizing your personal and professional brands. It takes effort, self-awareness, and a continuous habit of double-checking your message, tone, and topics across your brands.

Don't get too loose or comfortable with your personal brand. Save the family pictures and updates about your new puppy for your friends and family's social media handles. Blending or merging your personal brand into your more intimate circle of closest contacts and family members is a recipe for disaster. I already shared my election security experience. Once I realized that my defensive comments and angry responses might be snapped up and put on display by someone in the corporate or media world, I knew I had crossed a line.

Because of that episode, I drastically reduced my footprint on Face- book. Facebook wasn't an effective channel for either of my dual brands. While I could share media coverage where I provided tips to the average consumer on how to protect themselves in the digital world, most of my contacts on Facebook wanted to see pictures of new puppies and updates on how the kids were doing in school. Facebook wasn't their source for news or education, but I mistakenly believed it could be used for news and education.

Maybe it was also a manifestation of a bit of ego on my part. Having the benefit of a public platform and image and access to information that others didn't, there may have been a part of me that thought it was my "job" to educate others. It wasn't, and it still isn't. The less egotistical path opened when I realized that sharing knowledge and experiences is more effective than lecturing and teaching. And I was using personal social media as a pulpit.

Managing your social media posts, monitoring your language, and being conscious of how your tone may be interpreted takes a lot of mental energy and focus. It is also vital. You are integrated into each of your brands, and they are permanently connected once established. Think of that personal integration and connection between yourself and each of your established brands as an inter-permanent and symbiotic.   If one or the other of your brands begins to diverge away from the consistent pattern that has become the expectation of those who follow you, things will get weird. Let that divergence grow, and things will get bad.

I'll continue to emphasize this point throughout the book. This is why it is so important to recognize the fragility of your personal brand and how that brand can either augment or damage your professional brand. Your personal brand needs to have a separation from your personal life. Politics certainly has a place in your brand if you are a politician or elected official. For just about everyone else, avoid politics in your personal brand.

That's not to say that you can't have or display an opinion about current events or social issues. Leaders will always be looked to for their thoughts and observations on what is happening in their community or around the world.   Partisan politics can and will dramatically impact your career progression to micro-fame. I know a few personalities in various industries with very strong, visible political positions on both liberal and conservative ends of the spectrum. While they are all perfectly fine with the consequences of that choice, I can confirm that many people refuse to follow or interact with them precisely because of those views.

I realize this advice raises some questions and concerns. The people in the community who follow or listen to you have a say in the consistency of your brand. Frankly, they have a say in almost everything about your personal brand once you've established it. Should they be able to choose to follow or criticize you based on your political beliefs, family composition, or your position on social issues? I know we all want the answer to those questions to be no, but you already know the answer is yes, they can. And they will.

From amusement parks to beer to chicken sandwiches, we've all seen the consequences that taking strong positions can have for a brand. You aren't exempt from this reality. Your brand will be just as scrutinized, particularly as it grows. Crafting, managing, and sustaining your brands is all about how deftly you navigate the "third rail" issues that go on around us every day but have no relationship to our areas of expertise or field of interest.

Whoever wins the next presidential election rarely has a direct, immediate, or even lasting impact on what you are known for. The gears of government will always grind slowly for all governments and nations. The same goes for really challenging societal problems. What you are famous for and the expert knowledge you share is rarely associated with any of those problems.

I would be ecstatic if my knowledge of digital identity could make our world a better place for my children. I wish that my observations and recommendations about digital privacy would prevent people from being wrongly imprisoned and prevent governments from oppressing their people. If my presentations on digital consumer rights could eradicate theft, graft, human trafficking, and terrorism, I would work five times harder than I am right now. That just isn't how the world works.

You and I can use our joined personal and professional brands to create change in our small piece of this vast and complicated endeavor we call life.

THE AUTHENTICITY GRIND

Does authenticity really matter? Who determines if I'm authentic? And what can damage my personal or professional brand? In this chapter, we'll explore the role of authenticity and the common pitfalls that can undermine your brand's credibility.

The challenge of authenticity is a tricky one.

While authenticity might seem to belong to the three philosophical components of building a dual brand, it doesn't. Confidence, consistency, and trust are the silent influencers of our behavior and branding. When you have resolved to build your brands with those underpinnings, you will never wake up in the morning and think, "I need to make a post or write a blog today that exhibits my confidence, is consistent with my brand image, and people will then trust." Those three principles are like breathing. We don't think about them. We do them.

Unlike the three components I just mentioned, authenticity requires effort. More importantly, authenticity is what the professional world craves. In the world of experts and expertise, people subconsciously decide who they follow based on how authentic they perceive their expert. This is another one of those key differences between being an influencer and being an industry expert. Influencers can be (and many times are) inauthentic as hell. There are a lot of personalities out there who have no problem taking a check from any company that coughs one up. This is true even if the company's product or purpose does not align with who the influencer claims to be.

In the spirit of fairness, many celebrities and influencers are conscious and diligent about protecting their personal and professional brands. They are highly selective about the things, events, and moments they endorse. They put in the time, effort, and energy to ensure that what they stand for aligns with who they are and how they want the world to perceive them.

Terry Crews is the best human example of authenticity from which I've had the good fortune to learn. I love Terry. He is a wonderful, warm human being with sharp, professional instincts. Terry's high standards of selection in his endorsements exude authenticity. In a few conversations, he taught me so much about protecting your brand if you want a voice.

On paper, it is easy to think of Terry as a successful actor who used to play professional football and a guy who flexes his pectoral muscles now and then. Terry is a multi-talented juggernaut who may be one of the Zen masters of personal brand management. He surprises people by taking advantage of their disbelief or dismissiveness of his celebrity. Terry's personal and professional brands are very much the same. He studies and decides what gigs he will take, what products he will represent, and what causes he will champion.

He has frustrated his representatives and agents by stolidly refusing to attach his name to something he doesn't believe in. He is also one of the few true polymaths I've ever met. Terry is a visual artist, an actor, and a reality star. He is also a flute player, an athlete, a host, an announcer, a fantastic lip-syncher, and a man of strong, unwavering faith. There is no check on the planet with enough zeroes to make Terry turn his head and half-step or compromise his principles, beliefs, or brand.

I don't know this because I have watched or followed Terry for years and years. Nope. I had the good fortune of working with him when Ping Identity hired him to represent the Ping Identity brand. Terry became the "Chief Identity Champion" for Ping. I got the opportunity to spend quality time with Terry. We spent a lot of time together sharing stories and thoughts before recording podcasts and webinars for the company. I got to learn Terry's philosophies from the man himself. I don't believe I've met anyone who exemplifies the principles of authenticity as well as Mr. Crews.

Terry doesn't intentionally plan his moves to exhibit or amplify the appearance of authenticity. He reinforces his genuine authenticity by meticulously curating his personal brand. Terry won't represent certain products that don't align with his beliefs. He doesn't take on a role or job without researching what it takes to represent them well. While Terry has followers because he is an influencer, he also has those followers because he's an expert at personal brand management.

Terry told me that he never accepts offers to represent a brand, product, or cause that doesn't align with his beliefs and personality. He also shared that it drives his support team crazy when he refuses an offer that doesn't fit into his personal brand. Terry has agents, managers, and publicists, and he pays them to guide his career.

Even their expertise and experience won't induce Terry into making choices that he feels are irreconcilable with who he is at his core.

When I spoke with Terry and shared time with him, I had absolutely no doubt that the foundation of his beliefs and personal principles was developed long ago as a kid growing up in Michigan. He developed a work ethic that drove him to explore his interests in music, acting, playing football, and painting portraits of other NFL players. I'm continually impressed at the expansiveness of Terry's universe. Still, I'm much more impressed that he has built a fantastic life for himself while also diligently protecting and promoting his personal brand in a truly authentic way.

I can't itemize all the intangibles that go into being authentic. It is kind of like being tagged with that "expert" label. You don't get to decide whether you are authentic personally; everyone around you does. I suppose it is like being funny as a profession. Stand-up comedians can think they are humorous and do everything they are supposed to do to be funny. Ultimately, it is up to the audience, which registers the response, to determine whether a comedian is funny. Those philosophical pillars certainly play a part in being authentic, but not any larger part than your tone, delivery, language, or how you present yourself to an audience.

So, how does my authenticity manifest?

My perceived authenticity with my audience is most closely associated with how I speak. I've already shared a lot of storytelling advice, and how I speak isn't about the story but how I deliver it. As I've mentioned before, I am an extemporaneous speaker. Give me a picture, and I can tell a story without notes or teleprompters. This skill gives me a wide margin to be topically relevant in the moment and opens a palette for me to create things off the top of my head that catch the audience's attention.

One of my favorite examples of this happened during a keynote presentation I delivered a few years ago.

About halfway into my presentation, I had a slide that was a stock image of a hacker. Or rather, what the world thinks a hacker looks like. The picture was there to reference the annually escalating losses and increasing breaches and exploits occurring) in the digital world. However, when that slide popped up, I had a thought that simply jumped out of my head and through my mouth.

I looked up at the giant screen behind me on the stage, and there was the image: an indecipherable face staring at a laptop, fingers upon keys, wearing a hooded sweatshirt. I turned to the audience and said, "Hey, show of hands, who out there has ever seen a picture of a hacker that didn't have them wearing a hoodie?" The audience broke out into laughter. My brain didn't stop.

As the audience quieted back down, I said, "Yeah, that's my retirement plan. When I'm done doing this kind of stuff, I will start up a hoodie company and call it "Persistent Threat!"

Remember, the book is called "Famous with 12 People," so I do not expect anyone reading that story to understand why the audience started clapping, laughing, hooting, and hollering. It was a perfect reference for that moment, a nerdy cybersecurity reference that the couple of thousand people sitting in the hall completely understood. It was silly and preposterous, yet it spoke directly to the people gathered at this conference.

A large part of authenticity is about relatability. My audiences know I speak to and for them, not at them. They know I'm one of them because I speak the language, the vocabulary, and the idioms of our shared trade and craft. We've all experienced a moment where someone who professes to be a know-it-all about any given topic incorrectly uses one word or phrase. We cringe when it happens, and we immediately begin to question the authenticity of that person. Once your authenticity is in doubt, your entire message loses relevance with your audience.

Another brand characteristic that colors my speaking style resonates with my audience.

I curse—a lot.

Now, I'm not proud of this fact. I've tried to curtail my profanity. For the most part, I've been moderately successful. I'm not here to argue the effectiveness or appropriateness of excessively colorful language. In my case, so many people are familiar with this quirk that they worry about me if I don't let a swear word occasionally slip into the dialogue. Or at least they worry that I've sold out and I'm no longer authentic to my true self.

During one presentation, I stopped about 1/3 of the way through, looked up at the audience, and said, "I'd like to pause for a second and congratulate myself for not using any profanity so far. Many of you know I must work hard to make that happen."

There are plenty of studies that have recently been published that suggest that profanity is an effective way to communicate, and that Midwesterners are the most likely population to use foul language in the business world. Effectiveness aside, I agree with a study by the University of Cambridge that posits from a psycholinguistics standpoint that people who use profanity in a business setting are perceived to be more authentic than those who don't. Vital for me to mention I didn't adopt my potty mouth to be perceived as more authentic. No, the market hasn't discouraged me from utilizing my poor choice of words for so long that I've been enabled to continue those "bad" behaviors.

It isn't my profanity that mints authenticity, though. It is the perception of my audiences that this affectation is part of who I am. The colorful use of language on my part isn't meant to offend. I use this type of language, as most people use punctuation marks and bold text to emphasize the things that I feel are most important to convey in any given setting. Beat poets, musicians, actors, film writers, comedians, and even the occasional high-ranking member of state understand the power of foul language. Well-known people from each of these cohorts use off-kilter words to drive home important messages.

My mannerisms reflect that first principle of authenticity. Beyond the use of profanity, I am known for speaking bluntly. When something happening in my field of expertise is wrong, or another expert's observations are being maligned, my audiences know that I will speak up, speak out, and more than likely speak loudly about it. Whether "loudly" in a given circumstance is audibly or figuratively, my audience expects it from me.

One of the realizations I had as I learned more about this life of being a personality was that many industries or fields of practice have very little active debate occurring within their leadership circles.

The side effect this creates is that vast numbers of incredible people don't agree with the status quo positions of their peers and colleagues. But in an environment where everyone smiles, waves, and agrees, those same people have a hard time challenging all that group hugging and group thinking. Many of the personalities and experts in these very specific disciplines and endeavors are the people who have found a voice to question, critique, or poke holes in the current thinking of those fields. This reality has significant ramifications for your brand.

You are the voice. You are their voice.

It is possible that this component of "brand you" doesn't apply to your area of focus. While possible, I wouldn't say it is probable, though. Very few people are granted the expert label because they are doing what everyone else in their field is doing but doing it better. Olympic gymnasts don't win gold with the same routine their competitors do. They push themselves and their competitors to innovate and evolve. For those like Simone Biles, they push the very limits of what was thought to be possible by not listening to convention.

Mick Ebling is another amazing human and personality I have had the opportunity to learn from directly in person. He spearheads an incredible organization called NotImpossible Labs. In the context of being a voice for those who can't take a platform or speak to a market, Mick shared something valuable with me.

Everything that we know in this world that is currently possible was once considered impossible.

How will it ever become possible if someone isn't aggressively questioning the impossible? Questioning the impossible is confrontational, though. In the professional world, change is expected to be slow or non-existent. Change, whether we like to admit it or not, is the one thing that often feels impossible. When you are Famous with 12 People, you will almost always be an agent of change. You are seen as a thought leader, a pioneer, and sometimes even a troublemaker.

Shaking the cage of the impossible and poking the bear that is "the establishment" in your field is one of the most important ways to demand and drive growth and evolution in your professional world.

Supporting the status quo isn't interesting or inspiring and doesn't contribute to making what is currently considered impossible possible. I'm not suggesting you should march down to the next gathering of colleagues or post on business social media some bold declaration that you are a contrarian. We must keep that authenticity component in focus, right? But conventionalists don't make the impossible possible.

If you passionately believe that there are problems, challenges, deficiencies, or persistent failures in your area of experience, it is okay to use that as fuel for your brand. It is more than okay. You might feel like the only one who has ever thought about those issues in your field and how to improve things, but you are not. However, you can be among the few who stand up, speak up, and bring something different to the discussion. When you do, you become the voice for those who can't stand up and speak out. This type of leadership is a weighty responsibility.

Each time I have spoken, presented, or been interviewed, the more tangible the weight of that responsibility has been felt. Before the first word comes out of my mouth, I remind myself that these are my words and thoughts, but they can and should represent the people who have great ideas and a desire for change but don't have the microphone.

Being authentic in the micro-famous world comes with the obligation of being a voice for those in your community. While that may feel intimidating, this obligation has a serious benefit. Because of it, you will improve at what you do, how you present, what you share, and how you connect with others.

If there were one wish that I could fulfill for myself in the process of writing this book, it would be that I could find a way to express how to be authentic adequately. The number of times I have had people approach me and tell me how much they appreciated that I said what they felt needed to be said or that I made some bold statement about how the current situation in our community was wrong or unacceptable is uncountable. When you are authentic and true to yourself, it is almost a magnetic force. People are drawn to you. The power of authenticity is incredible, but the levers and mechanisms that produce authenticity are difficult to articulate.

Being inauthentic is a state that is much easier to describe. Perhaps knowing the behavior and language that will lead people to believe you aren't authentic can be more helpful than defining authenticity. We've already covered consistency at length, but many other flaws will result in your authenticity being questioned. Most of them you learned in elementary school.

Don't be a liar. Don't be a cheat. Don't be a thief. Don't be mean. Don't be cruel. Don't hurt other people.

There are many temptations in this world. It can be all too easy to lie when it is convenient or to steal other people's work and the mannerisms that have made them successful. It is easier to be a critic than a creator, meaning putting other people down or denigrating their ideas is much easier than creating new ones ourselves.

Hurting others reminds me of something Albert Einstein said, "Large minds talk about ideas; small minds talk about other people."

If we know the things that create an atmosphere of inauthenticity, we can at least look to the opposite end of the spectrum of those behaviors and actions to find hints of how to be authentic. As before, most of these things are learned when we are children.

Honor your word. Do what you say you will do. Give credit where credit is due. If it isn't yours, give it back. Treat others better than you'd like to be treated yourself.

Help others.

Being authentic is a grind. You must exert all your magical powers of self-awareness, consistency, confidence, and trust-building to achieve it. The market and your community will show little mercy if you fail to nurture your authenticity. While I may not be able to give you an easy recipe to follow so you can achieve or maintain authenticity in your efforts, The proof of authenticity is the presence of it in everything you do, not in some magic formula for who you manufacture it or create it. I hope I have at least proven how vitally important being authentic is to being famous with 12 people.

THE MYSTICAL POWER
OF SERENDIPITY

Isn't serendipity just another word for luck? What does it have to do with becoming micro-famous? And can I learn to spot those serendipitous moments? In this chapter, we'll uncover the difference between luck and serendipity and how recognizing these key opportunities can be crucial in your journey to micro-fame.

"The harder I work, the luckier I get."
– Samuel Goldwyn

I know many people who have tried unsuccessfully to find a path to being a speaker, personality, or expert. It can be tough and frustrating when you are eager, passionate, and want to break into this part of your career growth. Sometimes, you feel like the lead singer of a garage band trying to make it to the big league, but you can't even get a local gig. You tell everyone you know you are open and available to speak, present, perform, or talk. Yet for a while, maybe even for a very long time, no one takes you up on the offer.

An unfortunate side effect of the frustration many people feel when they experience these challenges is that they begin to think what they are missing is luck. But luck isn't a factor.

Serendipity is.

Serendipity is not luck, although many people firmly believe that it is. I didn't remotely understand the power of serendipity until I met someone who explained it to me and operated in the flow of it in a way that would completely change my life.

The Merriam-Webster definition of serendipity is gloriously precise; "the faculty or phenomenon of finding valuable or agreeable things not sought for."

I love this definition so much because it is so accurate. Serendipity isn't luck. It is a moment when you are presented with an opportunity or situation you weren't actively seeking. I also think there is a critical additive component to serendipity that requires your active participation and discernment.

Serendipity isn't a moment; serendipity is a choice.

People wish and hope for luck all the time.

"I hope I get lucky and win the lottery."

"I wish I could get lucky and score tickets to that sold-out show."

"I need luck like that guy; he didn't deserve that promotion."

Wishing and hoping are the channels we tune into when we want something we believe only luck can provide. But like Samuel Goldwyn said, the harder you work, the luckier you get. Maybe he should have said the harder you work; the more serendipitous things happen.

Serendipity manifests in our day-to-day lives way more frequently than luck does. Serendipitous things occur regularly for almost all of us. That frequency makes a huge difference in your career growth if you have tuned your senses to recognize it when it manifests.

I hope that by sharing several serendipitous moments from just the last couple of years, you can learn how to tune into the correct frequencies to recognize these moments in the moment. Music festivals, requests to be a guest on a podcast, the LA Times, and fitness conferences are all places and intersections in time where serendipity can happen. In fact, across all those events and venues, serendipity did happen.

My wife and I attended a music festival in Madrid, Spain, and asked a gentleman standing next to us if we could use the edge of his table to hold our drinks. He said "absolutely" instead of "si." Suddenly, there we were, striking up a conversation with a guy from San Antonio, Texas, before a set by Metallica in the middle of Spain. How does that even happen? We certainly didn't plan to meet a stranger who happened to be American from Texas and was as stoked to see Metallica as we were. There wasn't any luck at that moment. We weren't hoping and wishing we'd run into someone from San Antonio or his buddies from Austin there with him on their dream festival trip together as friends.

By the strictest dictionary definition of serendipity, we had found an agreeable thing not sought for.

This moment, though, is why I deeply and personally feel that the definition of serendipity is incomplete. The phenomenon, when experienced, requires a choice. That choice then determines what trajectory yours takes - or, sometimes, doesn't take. It could have a small impact on your life or an enormous one.   Your choice could simply result in a memory you share with a friend. "The weirdest thing happened in Madrid! We met a dude from San Antonio." When your friend asks, "And then what?" You responded, "Nothing, I just met a dude from San Antonio."

That isn't what happened to my wife and me, though. We spent the next four days hanging out with Joseph, Chuck, and Mike. We laughed, saved seats and tables for each other, and exchanged contact information. We discussed catching up at another music festival, maybe even creating a bigger group. We agreed to catch up for dinners and drinks while visiting each other's towns and cities.

I wasn't even remotely surprised when we learned Joseph and Mike worked in technology or that Joe and I had even worked for the same company at one point. Nope, that's serendipity. Something you weren't looking for finding you. Once serendipity presents itself, you get to make a choice.

We could have just told Joe, "Nice to meet you, thanks for the table." That would have been the end of it, right? We'd just have that pleasant little memory of meeting a guy from San Antonio. Instead, we chose to ask him why he came to Spain to see Metallica, Florence and the Machine, and The Pixies.

Serendipity is a choice. We chose to engage. Often, serendipity isn't just a choice precipitated from finding something agreeable you weren't looking for; it can be a series of cascading choices from that moment. Meeting our festival buddies is a great example of this dynamic.

Will we meet up with them again? Will we stay in contact after we exchange our personal information? Will we be bouncing up and down, singing our lungs out to Pearl Jam or Kings of Leon or Matt and Kim in the future? Will one of us introduce the other to a business partner, mention us to speak at a conference, or participate in a panel interview? No one knows for sure, but if we do, it is because we've all continued to make choices after that serendipitous encounter at a soccer field on the outskirts of Madrid.

What do music festivals and guys from San Antonio and Metallica have to do with your success in being recognized as an expert? Simply put, you must be attentive and constantly watching for those serendipitous moments. You must remain committed to choosing to follow the path that opens before you when something you weren't searching for lands on your doorstep. You might not open that door for a couple of years until, one day, you grab the handle. Then you look down, and lo and behold, waiting on that doorstep is an invitation to a meeting, a dinner, an event, or an interview.

Serendipity may be the most critical intangible item in your pursuit of being famous with 12 people. Once you begin to share your knowledge and experiences in the quest to help others, the number of serendipitous encounters you experience will exponentially grow.

I've been flying from my home to some destination to speak and struck up a conversation with a fellow traveler when the questions turn toward "So, what do you do for a living?" and I share that I'm a recognized personality in cybersecurity, serendipity almost always presents itself. The number of times those encounters have turned into more discussions, meetings, or magical opportunities is nearly countless. It is important to note this isn't just a one-way street of personal self-enrichment. I've met tour golf pros, movie stunt people, authors, guitar engineers, and welders who are all considered rock stars in their respective professions.

But again, serendipity isn't luck. Serendipity, while intangible, isn't effortless.

Thomas Edison said, "Success is 10% inspiration and 90% perspiration." Serendipity may be less of a percentage of perspiration in that equation, but it is still an event or moment that we must recognize, evaluate, and respond to on purpose. Sometimes, in minutes or even seconds, serendipity demands our active participation.

When serendipity manifests, you must be ready.

The number of serendipitous events in my life has accelerated since I started this portion of my career. Perhaps I've just become better at recognizing them.   I'm convinced that the cause for this acceleration is the active practice of storytelling, humility, consistency, and authenticity, which opens opportunities to grow and share expertise. As my brands have evolved, grown, and become more visible in the broader market, the most random opportunities I could imagine have materialized from nowhere. Something that I wasn't looking for just showed up. I think that's at the core of what Sam Goldwyn was saying. The harder you work on this effort to be FW12P, the luckier you become. Random conversations instantaneously convert into random offers for engagement and support.

One of many examples would be Oisin Lunny. He's a brilliant personality who has built an incredible brand for himself. He's a keynote speaker, musician, industry event emcee, and hilarious man. I ended up on one of the podcasts he hosts, and most people would assume that this happened because I reached out to him directly or that he contacted me. Neither was the case. I was standing on the floor of a conference hall here in the US when Mattias Berglund, the head of business development for a global device intelligence company, approached me. Mattias said he had seen my presentation at the conference and wanted to know if I would be up for joining his company's podcast, hosted by a guy who happened to live in Barcelona.

Would I like to be on a podcast for a company I don't know with a host in Europe? Serendipity demanded a choice, and the answer was yes.

Many times, what we think is serendipity is only a precursor or first stage to incredible opportunity. When I joined Oisin on his podcast, we had a fantastic time. My love of music is evident at this point. Well, Oisin has been in several bands in Europe. He has collaborated with artists like Depeche Mode, Sinead O'Connor, and Bono. He's on the advisory board for SXSW. His list of accomplishments and interests is longer than this book. I would have been happy just to file our interview away as a happy memory, but then Oisin reached out to me several months later. All he wanted to do was check in and say hello. No ulterior motives, no demands, or expectations were on his agenda. He was simply being authentic and relatable.

On the same trip where we met the guys from San Antonio, my wife and I were sitting at a sidewalk café enjoying sangria and reflecting on our trip up to that point. I said, "Wouldn't it be nice to hang it all up in Colorado, sell all our stuff, and buy a little bar in Barcelona?" While that might seem unbelievably random, it is consistent with how my wife and I live and dream. I told Marie that I knew a guy in Barcelona, and in a sangria-infused state of mind, I sent Oisin a note from my phone, saying we thought moving to Barcelona was a great idea. Almost instantly, Oisin texted back and said he'd be happy to

help us find a location and give us all the inside knowledge on becoming an expat in Spain. While we didn't directly take him up on his
offer, who knows? Maybe next year.

I recently sent Oisin another message to tell him that he inspired me
to start a music-based podcast. Again, he responded almost immediately and offered any help I might need. And, as serendipity does,
he let me know that he would be the emcee at a major conference in
my hometown that I just happened to be attending. Who knows what
will happen next when he and I grab a drink?

Recognizing serendipitous moments is a skill. Like all skills, when
practiced, you become better at identifying them. When you become
adept at recognizing them, you can immediately register that you are
coming face to face with a choice. Practice then makes you better at
making the more effective choices. Remember, there aren't any right
or wrong choices in that moment of serendipity. There are decisions
that yield different trajectories, not necessarily better or worse outcomes. It's kind of like making a choice when you are driving from
Manhattan to Los Angeles. You can go through the northern part of
the United States, the middle part, or the southern route. You will
still get to Los Angeles, but what you see, experience, and enjoy will
be vastly different depending on your chosen path.

How can you leverage serendipity in your career journey to be famous
with 12 people?

I've already covered, in substantial detail, that the most essential first
step is being aware of the dynamic and power of serendipity. There
are many different techniques and tricks that you can use to increase
the probability of serendipitous encounters. However, none of them
are helpful if you don't ascribe to or believe in the existence of serendipity to begin with.

As serendipity does, I was allowed to experience it in action again just this morning (or, instead, the morning I'm writing the draft for this book). My wife Marie asked me several months ago if it would be okay if she attended a Les Mills Fitness conference in Los Angeles. While not a serendipitous moment, I was presented with the choice to either be resistant and stubborn or flexible and agile. Considering the enormous number of conferences that I go to on an annual basis, it seemed petty of me to say anything other than yes and ask what I could do to make it happen. Given how much my wife supports my endeavors, I count myself fortunate to have the opportunity to support her in what she loves and is passionate about.

A couple of months after the decision was made and hotel points were used to grab a nice room directly across from the LA Convention Center where the event would be held, Marie asked if I would come along for the trip. Having a break in my work schedule due to the summertime lull in corporate America, I said sure. Then she asked if we could drive our camper van across the western states from Denver to LA and get some work done on our van at a great adventure van shop just north of the city. Again, these were not serendipitous moments in and of themselves but a series of choices that I could address with yes or no responses.

The travel week for the conference arrived, and we hopped in the van to begin our trek. Once we reached LA, we grabbed a rental car, dropped off the van, and drove to the hotel. We were settled in for a few days when I texted my nephew, Micah. Micah is a brilliant young artist who works for The LA Times. I'm biased, but he's an extraordinary human being. He always humbles Marie and me by asking for advice and guidance on various topics, ranging from what books to read to how to manage certain aspects of his budding career. Any chance we get to spend time with Micah, we enthusiastically take it.

I asked him if he'd like to meet us for brunch, and we caught up at a great soul food restaurant around the corner near our hotel.

Now comes the serendipitous part. While talking and enjoying our Sunday brunch, our server kept checking in on us. One thing I've learned about Los Angeles is that many people there aren't originally from Los Angeles. So, an effortless way to show interest in others is simply to ask them where they are from. Our server, Antoine, came by our table, and I asked, "Antoine, are you an LA local?" Antoine paused for a moment, probably because it isn't common for people to take a moment to ask someone about themselves these days. It is probably the most unexpected coming from strangers.

Antoine replied, "No, I'm originally from Cincinnati." His response immediately started a conversation around the table because Micah, my wife, and I were all originally from Ohio. I followed up with, "So, what brought you to LA?" Antoine told us he was a designer and illustrator and came to Los Angeles to pursue his art career. As serendipity would have it, sitting right across from me at the table enjoying brunch with us is my talented artist nephew, who works for the LA Times. He has already won an Emmy for his art contributions to a documentary and is exceptionally well-connected to the visual arts scene in Los Angeles. This moment of serendipity wasn't for my wife or me; it was for my nephew. After a round of questions and discussions about movies, personalities, and art, Micah and Antoine exchanged information with a promise to connect later.

Much like the serendipitous experiences I've shared with you, there are no guarantees that this encounter will lead to anything other than a coffee between Antoine and Micah. Or maybe it leads to something much more extensive, even life changing.

It isn't the future possibilities that I'd like you to consider, though. It's the action used to increase the possibilities and probabilities of a serendipitous encounter that matters. It was the outcome of choices that led to a moment.

It is easy to mistake this entire series of events for "networking." That is an entirely different endeavor. Serendipity can manifest while we are engaged in networking or among members of our network, but networking doesn't generate serendipitous moments by itself. Antoine is a nice young man who was our server for a moment on a Sunday in Los Angeles. A networking relationship would be improbable and unnecessary. I doubt that I would have anything valuable to contribute to Antoine professionally. I equally doubt that Antoine would have any time or interest in investing his energies into a guy from Denver just having biscuits and gravy in his station.

Networking and serendipity are not the same thing.

The action I took was what young Micah had shared with me and taught me several months before this moment. While discussing life and experiences under a tree in a park in LA, Micah talked about his journey from Ohio to Los Angeles and how, during a party, he was exercising his prodigious gift for small talk. The young lady he was talking to looked him in the eye and said, "You are just asking questions to have a conversation; you don't care about what I'm saying." Ouch.

Micah evaluated that assessment and told me that she was right. As a result, he chose to change that behavior. Micah told me that he started asking people questions about them. Not where they worked or what part of town they lived in; he asked questions like, "So, what are you doing to take care of yourself?"

I'm sure there is a brilliantly written book out there that offers the same advice: to truly connect with people, be empathetic, and be interested in them.

Now, those are superpowers we all have: empathy and genuine interest in another person. Well, maybe not all people have those superpowers. But these superpowers truly matter if you want to generate more serendipitous moments. I spent a lot of time thinking about Micah's story and revelation. I realized that in my own life, and most specifically in my move into micro-fame, I had accidentally been leveraging these superpowers for a long time. Not intentionally, not consistently, and not well in most cases.

No matter how brief the encounter, exhibiting a genuine interest in people you meet is like opening the door to a whole new thing. Not everyone is gifted with the natural ability to do this. It is far too easy and comfortable for us to meet someone and immediately orient the conversation to ourselves and our needs. Understanding the value of this approach is something that you can't unsee or unhear, though. You will feel your inner self tapping your shoulder from here on out. I hold myself accountable for trying harder each time I find myself in a setting where I'm meeting new people.

The more you and I practice empathy and genuine interest, the more intuitive our use of it will become.

Serendipity is finding something you weren't searching for. It is an amplifier for your career growth like no other. Once you've learned to recognize the moment when you are presented with it, I hope that I've given you some new tools to leverage and maximize the moment. I am forever grateful to have learned about this principle because of the amazing and incredible opportunities serendipity has offered me, not just in the past few years but for the entirety of my career.

I've covered quite a few of the philosophical components of being famous with 12 people, but there are a lot of tactical pieces to learn about and implement as well. We've still got a host of things to cover and add to your toolbox, like optimizing your use of social media, learning how to network effectively as an expert or aspiring expert, learning all the variations of content creation, and scoring media pickups.

THE NECESSARY EVIL THAT AIN'T THAT EVIL

———————

Which social media channels are worth your time? Do you even need to be on social media? And should you mix your professional brand with your personal profiles? In this chapter, we'll help you navigate the social media landscape, decide where to focus your efforts and explore the balance between personal and professional branding online.

———————

I issued a warning at the beginning of the book that I'd be tearing apart the topic of social media as part of the requisite components of being micro-famous. And here we are.

I wanted to address social media as a completely stand-alone chapter. While it is a vital component of your "brand you" marketing campaign, the tips and tricks and the risks with social media are a book unto themselves. As you are getting started or are in the middle of your journey to be famous with 12 people, there are a lot of basics to discuss about the role, impact, and problems with social media.

I want to be clear that the time and attention I can devote to this topic pales compared to the lessons and learnings people can acquire by following social media mega-experts in their field or hobby. What might be highly productive in a domain like investment banking may have no value in an area of expertise like mountain biking. While I can't give you specific guidance on the approaches that will work in your area of focus, I can share what I know and what I've learned so far in mine.

Before we dig into how social media can benefit and damage your brand efforts, it is worthwhile to talk about some structural challenges and problems with social media. It is also important to understand how the medium has grown to become the cultural monster that it is. I'm taking a bit of license on this topic because of what I do for a living. Cybersecurity, data privacy, and digital consumer rights are a big part of my everyday job, so I hope to have an informed opinion on this topic worth sharing.

From a historical perspective, social media has existed for less than a full generation in our lives, but it has become almost all-consuming in that same period. This suggests both the power and the risks of social media. Something that has grown so fast but is still so young has most certainly resulted in something like a 13-year-old boy who grows 8 inches over the summer. He seems destined for greatness because he's the tallest kid in his class, but he's also so unbearably awkward and uncoordinated that he is hard to watch. In full transparency, I was that 13-year-old kid. It automatically made me the center on my junior high school basketball team, where I was doomed to fail because I could barely walk upright. Thankfully, all my friends grew taller a year or two later and were way more coordinated, allowing me to fade from sports and focus on other endeavors gracefully. Let's hope social media grows a bit in the future, but I have doubts.

Social media has evolved from a tiny community of mostly tech nerds using basic bulletin boards accessed over internet connections. Those early social media forms seem glacial to today's technology users. They have also evolved into a ubiquitous influence on our lives, traveling at gig speed to devices that most people would have assumed were made by a superior alien intelligence if they had time-traveled from 2000 to now. I have watches that are more powerful than my first dozen cell phones and most of my desktops and laptops from the past. While it is easy to suggest that we just stop checking in on our social media channels and feeds, the reality is that social media is so entirely woven into our society that "checking out" is virtually impossible.

From a cybersecurity perspective, there is one simple design flaw in social media that shoulders the blame for why it has become such a toxic mix of all the worst characteristics associated with how humans interact. For some unknown reason, lost to the mists of time and decisions made by no known entity, the internet and the social media outlets associated with it were built with a considerable allowance for anonymity.

I speak on this phenomenon regularly, and what I share next are opinions you may disagree with. But I'd ask that you bear with me as I share these theories because they have an important relationship with how you should consider using and interacting with social media as a micro-famous person.

There isn't any other function or feature of human life where people expect and even demand anonymity. You can't walk into a local bank branch, stand in line at the teller, walk up to the counter, and demand money associated with your accounts without proving that you are who you say you are. From restaurant reservations to military service to getting into a concert or sporting event, nothing in our daily lives allows for or operates based on the principle of anonymity. When the internet began to incline toward everyday human interaction, though, it grew with a heavy inclination and a lot of support for allowing people (or artificial people in the form of bots and such) to be someone other than who they are.

Before I continue dissecting social media, let me take a beat. I fully understand that there are many places where anonymity is the only way to engage in self-expression, speak against oppression, or share information that many forces are trying to conceal. It would not benefit the point of this chapter or book to go into deep debates about whether several nations in this world at least nominally support freedom of speech and expression. However, it can at least be said that anonymity in countries and regions like the US and the EU has unfortunately provided greater facilitation of negative behaviors than it has of delivering tangible value in the fight for global freedom and equality. Sadly, the internet hasn't just facilitated a world of anonymous or falsely accredited commentary that can be mean, petty, inflammatory, and even incendiary. It has created a universe where this anonymous behavior comes with little to no accountability for actions or words.

Thank you for bearing with me during that brief philosophical journey through the ugly underpinnings of the internet. Here is why any of it matters about social media: First, you need to acknowledge the medium's power and purpose. Then, you need to be precise and thoughtful when using the medium.

Within the context of being famous with 12 people, you need to decide what social media tools you will use and define how you will use and interact with those channels. The personal rules you create for social media will be based on several of the principles already mentioned in this book, like authenticity, consistency, and credibility. Because, unlike the many thousands and even millions of people or technologies pretending to be people, you don't and won't have the benefit of anonymity. I mean, being anonymous while being mini or even maximally famous defeats the effort, right?

Now, let's move to how you can leverage the power of social media for your branding and amplify your voice in a crowded market filled with voices.

The most important thing to understand about any social media platform is that frequency, volume, and discipline matter. The most common misperception I discuss with other industry influencers and experts is, "I try not to post something every day because I don't want to be overexposed in the market." Well, that's not how social media platforms ever really worked, and it is light years away from how they work now.

Algorithms and AI selection routines constantly determine who should and shouldn't see whatever you've typed into the little box, even for what you think are bland or boring posts. How frequently you post doesn't matter because frequency and volume don't determine what gets seen or by whom. The real driver for that is keywords associated with your viewers. Sometimes, the social media user can explicitly determine or define those keywords.

I track several keywords on LinkedIn and Twitter that focus on new posts about computer hacks, breaches, and other cybersecurity-related events. That is the kind of nerdy thing I'm into. You might be into words tied to economic trends, specific brands, or other world events. Even if you don't specify what words you are interested in, those magical algorithms do it based on your posts, reading, and patterns.

This results in only some of the followers you have, or non-followers, seeing some of your stuff some of the time. You can post 3 or 4 times a day, and there is no certainty that everyone in your network will see any of those posts, let alone all 3 or 4. It is hard to fathom that sometimes social media isn't personal but contextual. You aren't creating content; you are a part of the context-based experience where another person's interests, passions, problems, focus, and fascinations are a bigger part of the equation than how many times you post in any given period.

In the spirit of love, I must tell you it is time to get over yourself and how frequently you post on social media. It isn't about you; it is about what you have to say. And some people will see it, while other people won't. Having discipline and understanding how to work the system will increase the probability of getting your content in front of people who aren't directly in your network. Ultimately, that's the goal.

Another interesting debate about social media is whether to post in short or long form. I follow a lot—and I mean a lot—of micro-famous people on social media platforms. When it comes to how you should use social media, there is only one correct answer. That answer is whatever form you choose that gets results and speaks to the audience you are trying to communicate with on the platform.

There are many great experts in my industry, such as Chris Roberts. Chris is a corporate Chief Information Security Officer who usually writes mini-blog posts on social media. They are profound and pithy, and everyone is a nugget of guidance for the cybersecurity industry. Chris has more than 46,000 followers on LinkedIn, which is enormous for that platform. People interested in what Chris has to say have no problem with his longer format approach to posting.

I know an entire army of experts who prefer to use Twitter/X as their chosen communication channel. By design, short-format writing is a requirement on platforms like Twitter/X, Threads, and Mastodon. Another example from my area of expertise is Dmitri Alperovitch, the co-founder of Crowdstrike. Dmitri isn't just a multi-billion-dollar start-up founder; he's also started a think tank, is a senior fellow for the Harvard Belfer Center, and holds many board positions. Dmitri is a master of the short form of social media with a couple hundred thousand followers. I'd like to think he's just a short-form ninja because how in the heck does he have the time for any kind of long-form communication?

Short and long-form messaging are both effective. It comes down to which is the most effective for you and which you can best use to build a dependable pattern of creation. In my case, I've learned that I'm mostly consistently in the medium form space. I try to be conscious of the value of the economy and the accuracy of words. One of my favorite quotes of all time is from Mark Twain; "The difference between the almost right word and the right word is really a large matter. 'Tis the difference between the lightning bug and the lightning."

I find the short format platforms too limiting from a character perspective. Twitter/X, Mastodon, Threads, and other platforms have historically limited the number of characters allowed. In the case of Twitter/X, differentiating the character count is based on paid or unpaid accounts. I used to think that the character limitation was what bothered me. In hindsight, I think the real problem I have with short-form social media channels is that I find the user experience of reading on these platforms frustrating. Given the hundreds of millions of people that use these platforms, I fully embrace the possibility that this shortcoming has more to do with my reading and perception style than any flaw in the short-form social media platforms.

Posting length is a preference, with neither short nor long form having any distinct advantage over the other. The only advantage comes from the capability of the writer to express themselves in a way that their audience desires and appreciates. There are a lot of different components to social media to consider beyond the platform or platforms you use and the length of posts you make. To put additive fuel in your social media engine, you must address mechanical items that will expand the number of eyes and views you capture for whatever you post.

My goal for many of the topics in this book is to introduce you to some basics and concepts that I've learned on this journey. The body of knowledge about increasing your follower count or maximizing your post performance is vast. I always dig into those resources to learn new things and achieve both outcomes. I apologize if my suggestions are basic or obvious to more experienced social media users. I hope you share that deeper knowledge with others in your community of influence.

Another critical component of social media management is imagery. A picture is worth a thousand words, as the adage goes. Social media proves that. Studies, analyses, and surveys over the last decade show that social media posts with visual images attached outperform text-only posts by anywhere from 30% to 80%. That's a sizable improvement, and even more so when you consider that you may be posting several times a week. It's like compound interest, in a way. The more you drop posts with images, the larger the audience for each post and the larger the cumulative total views you will acquire each week.

My experimentation with images has helped me confirm what should be obvious, but I'm a slow learner sometimes. The most crucial bit of learning is that images that connect to the topic create better results. Duh. I know, right? But this isn't as easy to pull off as you might think it is. Many of us in this micro-famous community work in fields of endeavor that are abstract in concept to vast numbers of the human population. It is hard to develop a picture that ties to something industry-specific, like a fraudulent account takeover or an API security exploit.

Chip and Joanna Gaines of "Fixer Upper" fame can easily find or create an infinite number of relatable images to support their social media posts. Home improvement is tangible and visible. There is an old, dilapidated kitchen today, and then "bam!" Tomorrow, there is a gorgeous makeover. There is a real shortage of meaningful images in career fields like insurance, medicine, physics, or banking. This is why, in cybersecurity, we are terminally stuck with thousands of pictures of the same dude in a hooded sweatshirt with matrix-like neon symbols cascading behind him. Now you can see why I'm starting that hoodie company.

Depending on your career field, you may need to get creative with image generation to emphasize your post. Once you start creating images, you also must navigate the occasionally frustrating world of being conscious of copyright and citation demands. Screen captures or downloads of "free" images online can become a minor mess if you aren't mindful of copyrights and trademarks. You need to be considerate of the work of others for imagery that may not truly be in the public domain. Just because an image or a meme has been posted on the internet a bajillion times doesn't mean it's legal or appropriate for you to grab it and use it how you see fit. This is even more so when you have some visibility as a micro-famous person. If you are a recognized brand, it is easy to find you if a cease-and-desist order needs to be delivered.

When hunting down the right image for a post, I pay attention to image sources and trademark-protected brands. If I find an irresistible image I have concerns about using, I do an image attribution in my post, either crediting the source (like the New York Times) or the artist or creator. This situation doesn't happen frequently. Usually, I can find a suitable image that doesn't come with worries about usage. You should give credit where credit is due, though, in cases where you need to use someone else's art. You can also look at subscription image services. Paying for the right to use images from organizations like Shutterstock or Alamy alleviates the risks you face with copyrighted or protected materials. I've used Shutterstock off and on over the last several years, but generally only during periods of posting or content creation that are heavily dependent on images. These image services aren't cheap but can be very effective when needed.

The second thing I've learned about visuals is that when in doubt, humor never hurts. In many cases, humor is the right thing to juice a post to stratospheric levels. The world of memes and GIFs must be inhabited by some of the most ridiculously creative and instantaneously reactive humans ever to exist. It seems like the digital ink barely dries about an event, and people have crafted the most impressive and absurd visuals in the moment.

Tools like Meme Generator and MemeCreator allow you to create your own industry or field-specific memes. Creating your own humorous visuals can be powerful if you have the gift of being funny, dry, wry, or witty. For example, the number of stand-up comedians specializing in cybersecurity is probably near zero. But the number of funny people I've met who work in cybersecurity is uncountable.

You and I know the language of our respective career fields, the inside jokes and the obscure ironies, and the quiet parts that people are afraid to say aloud. That knowledge can be powerful when applied to making visuals. I am obsessed with finding ways to use Will Ferrell in the scene from Anchorman: The Legend of Ron Burgundy' where he's in a telephone booth screaming, "I'm trapped in a glass case of emotion!" The same is true of Steve Carrell riding a grizzly bear in the same film.

My final learning about visuals is that no image may be more powerful than the one you take or create yourself. We live in a society with a camera in every hand and every pocket. I'm ceaselessly fascinated by the quality and creativity people display in the photos and videos they take. Many micro-famous people I know and follow can inspire and perfectly explain critical concepts in their areas of expertise with the images they create and share. This means you might have to up your game in this area if it is the path you choose for your visuals. I think we all know people who are smartphone-camera-illiterate. Some of those people might be us. For every heart-stopping mountain sunset, there are 1,000 horrible group selfies. I don't have research to back those numbers up, but I think I'm being conservative. Quality is a component of consistency, and a bad image associated with your post can kill the vibe faster than just about anything.

Once you've learned the basics of short and medium-format and image-enhanced tips on engaging with your social media platforms and followers, it is time to consider a more advanced handful of dynamics as you grow your online presence.

Search engine optimization, or SEO, is the hidden neural network of social media and the online world. Many of us have heard about it, but few outside the universe of digital marketing specialists know how to master it. Few of us even know how it works. I don't pretend to know the intricacies or the science behind this mechanism, but I fully understand its importance. And you need to as well.

Words matter—really matter—on the internet. Words are how people find you. This is true for the broader World Wide Web and social media platforms.

Each of these channels, and others, have embedded search engine capabilities that the curious among us use to find content, contacts, and services. While I didn't mention it in the chapter on securing your name (or a variation of it) as a domain, you should be able to immediately see how valuable a "name" URL can be in improving searches for you on the internet. Search engines crawl the internet, constantly looking for words and knitting those words together into something like a fabric. Your name is a word (or words). Events, places, moments, activities, news articles, white papers, and social media postings are all formed from words on the internet. Video may be a different form of content, but embedded within those videos are words and phrases.   One of the highest-order priorities for search engines that place you on the first page of a search return is a domain name.

If you Google "Richard," "Bird," and "identity" right now, I should be the majority of the first, second, and third pages that you get back as a response. The same goes for my name and "cybersecurity" or my name and "API security." The association of my focus areas with my name isn't coincidental, and it isn't luck. It is work. It also involves knowing how the system works. Some of these associations happen organically over time. The more you write, post, blog, vlog, and podcast, the more accurate the information that search engines accumulate into a profile about you. But you must also learn how to weave the specific words that represent you, your views, and your unique knowledge into everything you create and post online. This is another place where consistency of your message and positions comes into the picture.

I use essential keywords and terms that will effectively signal search engines in almost every piece of content I create, every media quote I provide, or every keynote presentation I give. I don't have to intentionally check whether I remembered to add those words to anything I create. At this stage in my journey, it is entirely automatic. The magic words are identity, API security, cybersecurity, data privacy, and a few others. If I were inconsistent in applying these words and a few others, I would make it much harder for search engines and web crawlers to do their jobs. The constant use and consistent application of these words in association with my name is the secret sauce in amplifying my web and social media presence.

I benefit from knowing which words are the most valuable in my profession. I know what my audience and followers will be searching for and what people I haven't been introduced to yet are searching for. When a news story pops up about a specific kind of cybercrime, someone searching for information on that event has a much higher probability of finding my name in their search returns. It might be easy to believe that this is only system manipulation on my behalf.

It is not.

I'll say it repeatedly: you have something important to say and share in the "out there." Expanding your audience isn't about growing your influence but sharing your knowledge. Don't be ashamed to capitalize on the web and social media mechanics to grow your audience. The more you learn about the power of keywords and fundamentals like search engine optimization (SEO), the more avenues and opportunities you can and will create to share your knowledge.

You aren't just limited to the words that float around the internet. The nice thing about social media platforms is that you can create your own words! Not imaginary or nonsensical words, though. You can create your own catchphrases or word associations. Hashtags, handles, and other doodads and gadgets in the social media basket are helpful tools to boost that word association game and craft brand-specific words that are yours.

I mentioned that on LinkedIn and Twitter/X; I use the handle or hashtag #theguywiththebowtie. Using this hashtag allows me to flag my posts and improve the probability that they will manifest in the feeds and views of people who follow me. It also is a phrase that connects my real-life persona and my digital persona. Wearing bow ties for some of my presentations and keynote speeches reinforces the digital handle. Using the digital handle embeds the imagery in the minds of my followers, colleagues, and peers.

Creating your hashtag isn't a requirement, but it can be fun and valuable. It is only one of many methods you can use, but their goals are the same: improving the odds that something you've written, posted to your website, or shared on a social media platform gets seen by just one more person.

Sometimes, the variety of methods and tricks can seem overwhelming. This chapter only covers images, words, and content types. There is an entire science behind things like post timing. You can use the internal reporting tools on several platforms to pinpoint the best time, day, and date to publish a post. Post timing is, like all the recommendations in this chapter, a tool and not a guarantee. However, post timing also opens up the world of automation.

You can pre-write posts on many platforms and schedule them for publishing on those ideal days and times. Pre-writing is a powerful method for increasing your social media output volume. Rather than only posting when the inspiration strikes you, you can build up several posts and give them little wings, releasing them into the wild on your chosen schedule.

Automation isn't limited to just the platform features of your social media channels. You can pay subscriptions for other solutions that help you curate content, schedule posts, and manage many other components of your social media strategy. Finding the best tools for you takes a bit of sorting and research. The digital marketplace is filled with several options that don't work for just one person as they are intended for organizations with marketing departments that employ social media engagement professionals. There are dozens of these solutions, but the companies that most people are familiar with are Hootsuite, Loomly, MeetEdgar, and Zoho Social.

These tools can get spendy for the average person. With monthly subscription rates of $10, $20, or even more per month, it is easy to rack up several hundred dollars of cost in a year for these services.   I have tried a couple of them over the past few years. As my discipline around social media posting improved, I found myself outgrowing the need for these platforms' support. I can also see a future where I might need to re-subscribe to one. When you consider the availability and limitations of your capacity, there is an unavoidable bit of math that impacts us all. Everything in life is a factor of time and/or money. When my bandwidth is stretched too thin with other activities to support, grow, and develop my personal brand, I'll change the tools I use to manage my output.

Social media isn't evil. It is agnostic.

How you choose to use social media and how any of us choose to use it determines the value and damage it can deliver.

Social media is necessary on the journey to being famous with 12 people. The ubiquity of social media makes it unavoidable. The recommendations I've made and shared with you are personal learnings, but they only scratch the surface. I encourage you to find your preferred tools, platforms, and formats. Take the time to evaluate which of them works best for your message and your personal style. Ensure that you don't spread yourself too thin. Mastering a social media platform will be more effective than just being okay with all of them.

Building your brand isn't a purely digital affair. You have work to do in the real world, hands to shake, and friends to make around the globe and down the street. Building and growing your network is your next step.

Networking isn't just about adding to the number of people who know and follow you. It is about finding and expanding your community. That community will be filled with people who will become your biggest advocates and provide you with opportunities and resources to succeed in your efforts.

NETWORK EFFECTS

Networking is worth its weight in gold but takes just as much work to mine and refine.

Networking is another topic on which I cannot claim expertise but will explicitly declare its value. Networking is vital to strengthening all the key components of pursuing your passion for becoming an internationally recognized expert in something no one cares about. The size and quality of your network are the foundation for being famous with 12 people.

As with many of the factors and skills I've mentioned, many resources are available to help you get better at networking. Sharing what I've learned should only add to those great resources. I hope I've also gained some unique knowledge about the subject that will help and inspire you to grow this talent.

Networking is a funny enterprise. Over nearly 40 years of intentionally or unknowingly engaging in the practice, I've seen every variation and flavor of how people network. Sadly, many believe networking is simply meeting people and expecting things to happen. Even with all the resources available to learn how to be a great networker, the truth is that a considerable percentage of the professional world sucks at networking. Many people fall into the "mass retail" version of networking. They know an enormous amount of people, but that's it. Nothing material, interesting, or valuable ever comes from it. Knowing people for the sake of knowing people is something, but it's not networking.

Networking has gotten even more convoluted and confusing with the rise of business social media. The LinkedIn Open Networker (LION) effect has taken the "mass retail" networking professional and added a nuclear-powered engine. Amassing thousands upon thousands of connections without a plan or purpose for invoking a network's power is a strange hobby. It also serves as a proof point of the disconnected reality of social media. Much like our personal experiences on platforms like Facebook, being "connected" to someone does not mean we are real friends, business associates, partners, colleagues, peers, mentors, or mentees. It just means we clicked an "accept" button when an invitation arrived in our notifications.

Having a robust network isn't the same as having a lot of LinkedIn connections.

When I was a young tech professional just getting started, I used to attend every networking event I could. Being in technology, I was also an early adopter of just about every platform that came along. Without anyone as a role model or mentor to teach me how to propagate and grow a healthy network, I simply tried to make as many connections as possible, as often as possible. It wasn't an effective strategy.

Many people are keen to blame digital channels and social media for the downfall of our species being able to connect in genuine and honest relationships. That inclination is certainly revisionist history. In the days before social media, I can tell you that networking events were in person, well attended, and just as ridiculously awkward as any interaction today on Slack or LinkedIn. Networking requires a certain, and sometimes substantial, capacity for socializing. Being social and engaging with members of society. You know, like communicating with people and not talking at them.

Communicating is a combination of skills that must be practiced, honed, and perfected.

Before someone criticizes that "nothing can be perfect," let's pause to think about the world of absolutes. If nothing can ever be perfect, then the state of imperfection must not be achievable either. If perfection is an absolute, imperfection must be an absolute as well. In both directions, these are the far ends of the perfection-seeking spectrum, and one can't exist without the other. We've all learned that imperfection isn't just possible; it is a regular condition of many aspects of our world and lives. Perfection is, too, but we don't see it as frequently because it takes work and practice to achieve that specific state.

Imperfection requires little to no work or effort. That's why it is so abundant. When it comes to practicing and perfecting specific skills and the conversation turns to "there's no such thing as perfect," I'm reminded of the scene in Office Space (possibly the best American business documentary of all time – young readers, if you haven't seen it you have to make it happen) when Lawrence asks Peter what he'd do with a million dollars.

Lawrence, played by Dietrich Bader, asks, "Well, what about you?"

Pete Gibbons, played by Ron Livingstone, replies, "Nothing." He adds, "I would relax... I would sit on my ass all day... I would do nothing."

Stunned, Lawrence replies, "You don't need a million dollars to do nothing, man. Take a look at my cousin! He's broke, don't do shit."

Imperfection takes no effort. I'm not discounting that there are more than a few people in the business world who expend a ton of effort to achieve imperfection. I think that dynamic is a topic for an entirely different book than this one. Suffice it to say, though, many of the topics in this book require practice, and networking is included in that list. These skills won't get better by doing nothing.

Perfection rant, over. Back to networking.

It is important to acknowledge that the problems with networking today aren't problems with technology development and its mass user adoption. Neither is the ubiquitous access to social media platforms or those platforms' failures to actively discourage bad behavior, poor form, and horrible manners. The awkwardness and disconnect we feel when trying to network in person or online reflects who and what we are as a species.

In my experience, the percentage of people who are fluidly confident in all the flavors of social interaction and comfortable striking
up conversations with total strangers is tiny. Even when you come
across someone with these capabilities, you often learn that they are
just as fragile, dysfunctional, and clumsy (in their minds) as you are
(in your mind). Like many of us, most of these people are functional
introverts.

When I tell people that I'm a functional introvert, they never, ever
believe me.

"But you can tell stories for days!"

"You aren't shy!"

"Once you start talking, you never shut up; you can't be an introvert."

Each of these statements is very true. I do have a lot of stories, I'm
not particularly shy, and I talk way too much, but none of these
characteristics have anything to do with being an introvert. Intro-
version and extroversion are manifestations of our personality.
Do we like to be in a small, controlled universe where we can feel
comfortable being ourselves? Or do we want big, populated events
or occasions where we can feel comfortable interacting with others?
I prefer the former.

I prefer small settings where I can be open and honest with people
I trust and enjoy spending time with. Talking and storytelling are
more of a defensive mechanism than a social skill. It took me years to
realize that my self-conscious mechanisms guided me to tell stories
rather than talk about how I felt or thought about certain subjects
when socializing.

I'd much rather be in a quiet corner at a busy event talking to the few folks I know than shuttling around the party, shaking hands, and making small talk. I am always in awe of people who are masters of small talk. A lot of us cringe at that term, small talk. It is regarded as useless, vacuous, and silly, which is precisely what anyone would think about small talk if they sucked at it.

So yeah, if you hate it, I will say it. You probably suck at small talk. I know I do.

People who have mastered this talent are worth your attention. They are like magicians, with some cool card tricks as conversation start-ers. Like everything I've shared in this book, small talk is learnable and well worth your effort of practice and learning. First, though, we must address the whole introvert/extrovert thing.

If large percentages of the human population are introverts, then the most important news is that you are not alone! This phenomenon is super important. We tend to wander through our lives believing we are a singularity. No one has the same problems as us. No one has the same fears as us. No one has the same hardships, challenges, or issues as us. You eventually realize the more time you spend with people, the more you learn that you are not alone. In anything.

You were embarrassed a long time ago because you forgot your lines in an elementary school play, and now you can't imagine standing up and talking to a room full of people. Yeah, 17 other people like you are at this event or that conference. Do you think you can't get up in front of your peers at your company's quarterly sales meeting because of the karaoke performance you flubbed at the holiday party last year? There is probably a busload of people in your company who did the same thing.

This karaoke example is very personal. I have a peculiar habit and need to bomb on stage with a karaoke performance of anything by the Black-Eyed Peas, KC and the Sunshine Band or Miley Cyrus regularly. It isn't healthy.

You are not alone in your awkwardness! Or in your fears! Everyone around you, except for a few natural extroverts, struggles with the same roadblocks as you regarding networking and socializing. So, stop using it as an excuse. I use this truth as an enabler. When circulating at networking functions, my entry maneuver of choice into a conversation that may be happening is to walk up to the group and listen for a minute. Then, at a non-awkward (or less awkward) moment, I say, "Hey, the goal of these kinds of things is to get out and meet people and discuss great ideas. I'm bad at this, so I thought I'd disclose that up front so we can find something mutually interesting to discuss." This little trick is a huge icebreaker. I'm saying how almost everyone in the conversation is feeling. These kinds of tricks permit everyone in the conversation to be awkward, which is liberating.

We've established that you are not a lonely, tiny starfish in a vast ocean all by yourself when it comes to networking and socializing. You are not unique in your awkwardness or discomfort in social settings. That knowledge and self-awareness alone are enough to improve your networking performance immediately. Still, there are a few other ideas and notions that I'd love to share with you to help you up your chances of serendipitous events happening.

Oh, I forgot to tell you why networking is so important. Networking increases the probability of serendipitous things happening in your life! We know by now that serendipity is a massive accelerator for being famous with 12 people.

As seems to be the case while I'm writing this book, I had another serendipitous moment just yesterday. I flew to Las Vegas for a 30-minute presentation at a major conference. One thing you must get used to in this micro-famous world is that not every speaking engagement is a room filled with hundreds or thousands of people. My speaking time slot was sadly aligned with the conference happy hour in the last round of presentations on the first day. That is a bad combination. The clock struck the minute of my starting time, and in a vast hall set up for probably 400 people, there were about 18. When you've spoken as much as I have, you typically assess that situation and say, "Well, at least 18 came for the show." So off I went and started sharing knowledge.

After the presentation, I walked through the hall and back to the exhibitor's area when a gentleman approached me and said, "Columbus, Ohio!" Yep, I'm in Vegas, so that was random. He stuck out his hand and said, "I'm Robert Brzezinski, and I saw you speak more than five years ago." We talked about that presentation and the one I'd just made, and then I asked Robert about what he was doing now. His professional focus had turned to working with Microsoft technologies. I told him that he should let me know if he ever had any problems or issues with any of the Microsoft products he was implementing for his customers. I'd connect him directly with my colleagues and friends in those product areas.

A genuinely serendipitous moment presented itself at that networking event. One that not only opened an avenue for me to further help someone in the future but also gave me a big boost personally as a speaker. It was encouraging to know that more than five years before that conversation, I had said something that would stick with a person and have meaning for them.

After years of doing this FW12P thing, I don't have the option to tell people I don't have time for them at networking events and conferences. Especially people who follow me or have seen me at other events. Would I have loved to have returned to my hotel room and rested or gone to dinner with my team? Sure. But defaulting back to my introverted self would have eradicated the possibility of several serendipitous moments that happened yesterday.

Another networking trick I love comes from one of my mentees, my nephew, Micah Fluellen. Yes, I'm talking about the same Micah from the restaurant in the chapter about serendipity.

Micah and my youngest son have been friends since the womb. My late wife and our best friend Jan were pregnant simultaneously with Micah and Xavier. Micah's father, Jeff, is my most trusted friend. To have Micah call me "Uncle Richard" is a humbling honor, and he's one of my own in that regard. Both boys have grown and flourished in their young adult lives, but Micah has had an exceptional career track. Before he turned 26, he had already earned his first Emmy Award.

Micah lives in Los Angeles. He moved there just before the COVID pandemic to work for the LA Times. Location-wise, he is right in the heart of entertainment and media, and he has participated in an incredible array of projects with many different creators and outlets in LA. Whenever I am in LA, whether for work or fun, I go out of my way to find an opportunity to spend time with Micah.

I mentioned the following story about Micah in a previous chapter, but it bears repeating here in more depth.

One morning, we had the time to meet in a local park and talk about life and work while sitting under a tree and soaking in the Southern

California sun. Micah and I talked about networking and his experiences at parties and events interacting with other artists. Networking is the lifeblood of the creative community. Any given conversation can lead to the next gig or a new job. Micah felt he'd been doing a good job of making all the right connections in Hollywoodland. Then, he shared a conversation that changed his entire perspective on how to interact with people in a meaningful and memorable way.

Micah said he was at an event, making the circuit around the venue to meet and talk with people. Micah is one of those natural extroverts I mentioned earlier. He's the fearless type in all the possible variations of the term. So, approaching people and starting a conversation isn't a problem for him. Micah said he approached a young lady and began talking with her.

"What do you do?"

"Where do you work?"

"What types of projects are you focused on?" Micah said he asked all his standard playbook questions, but something odd happened.

The young lady looked at Micah and said, "You don't care what my answers are; you are just doing what you think you are supposed to."

Micah said he was initially shocked, but then he thought about it and realized the young lady was right. He had perfected the mechanics of networking but not the meaning.

I asked him, "So, you learned something. What did you do with what you learned?" He shared a suggestion I think is so valuable and incredible that I can't help but encourage everyone I know to try it.

Micah said, "I started asking people at these events and parties, 'What do you do to take care of yourself?'" He built out that repertoire to include non-invasive but mindful questions about why and not where you work.

"What inspires you in your work?"

"Do you want to do this type of animation for a long time, or is there something else you are passionate about?"

"What was the last trip or adventure you took that opened your mind to something new?"

These are the kinds of questions that motivate people to share their stories, dreams, and ideas. They are also the kinds of questions that show a genuine interest on your part in the other person. These questions don't scratch the surface of a person's interests. They open the door to a deeper understanding of who someone is and why they are pursuing the goal or opportunity they are chasing. It is this beginning of a personal connection that amplifies the power of a network. The added power of these questions in networking environments and relationships is that they exponentially increase the probability of a serendipitous event. By engaging in networking from this approach, you are learning how you might be able to contribute value to another person's endeavors.

So, this is the secret. A poorly concealed secret, given all the networking books that have been written about this principle. A powerful network is an exchange of value between humans, but the offer to begin that type of relationship comes from you. It comes from understanding the other person's goals and focus so that you can use your broader network of arms, legs, ears, eyes, and brains to help them attain their desired outcomes.

Over the years, I've had many opportunities to see this dynamic in action. I had learned to do the same thing Micah had years before, but I had never been able to articulate it as precisely as he did. I have both initiated and been the beneficiary of instantaneous offers for help.

"I know someone in the industry; let me connect you with them."

"Why don't you come by my office? We can discuss what you think is missing in the market today to solve this problem."

"I know the right person to help you with that problem; I can connect them to your HR department."

These types of actions and engagements aren't rare at all in my various networks. Their active prevalence reflects the people in these networks' higher-level awareness about how to contribute value to others.

If I could make a decent living out of just connecting people with other people in my network, I would jump at that job in a minute.

The digital world and social media do not diminish the relevance or effectiveness of these techniques and core principles for networking. If we, as a collective community, agreed to use these platforms exclusively for good and contributing value, they could be even more effective than in-person networking. I've already articulated many of the foundational problems with social media. Hence, the reasons we can't seem to get our act together and leverage these technologies to improve networking relationships are clear. Sure, it's sad that we take the most significant accumulation of knowledge, talent, and information and weaponize it to bully, bloviate, and alienate other human beings. That still doesn't negate the truth that these platforms still have the potential to be way more useful tomorrow than they currently are.

I engage in value contribution conversations on LinkedIn all the time. Probably two or three times a week.

"Hey, would you mind introducing me to Bob?"

"Can you join this podcast?"

"Do you know anyone in this space that I could ask some questions for my new book?"

Lately, Slack has created even more compelling network-related interactions for me. Recently, I've been a volunteer advisor for a start-up company. My colleagues and friends who are a part of this founders' journey are all on a Slack channel together. It is a brilliant way to exchange ideas, ask for help or guidance, and crowdsource the encounter like a digital happy hour. Everyone else might not have a cocktail on the channel, but I am.

Networking begins with committing to being a value-contributor to other people, especially those you've only recently met or haven't met yet. The network you build becomes the launch pad of your voice in the market. By mastering the craft of networking and socialization, even if it doesn't come to you naturally, you greatly improve the probability that you will find something you were searching for. You will be in that flow of serendipity.

MAXIMUM FLEXIBILITY

Wait, I might have to pay to become micro-famous? Can't I just expect people to respect my time? You want me to show up where, when? In this chapter, we'll dive into the realities of building micro-fame, including the investments—both financial and personal—that are often required to seize the right opportunities and grow your influence.

Sometimes, everyone wants you everywhere.

If you continue to grow your brand successfully, you will get many opportunities to speak, meet, present, socialize, and attend various events. Even if you don't find your brand growing, you will be taxed by the ever-expanding steps and efforts you take to fix that problem.

Maximum flexibility is the secret weapon when it comes to achieving FW12P.

My favorite example of this dynamic and superpower is content creation. At the beginning of this book, I said that writing is a less critical but still important requirement for your personal and professional branding efforts. Sometimes, people conflate the terms "writing" and "content creation." Writing can be a content creation outlet for you, but it isn't the totality.

Over the last few years, blogging has given way to vlogging and other forms of video-capture expression. This has dramatically displaced the need for sitting down and typing out pithy thoughts and observations in written form while opening the aperture (pun intended) for visual methods of communication with your audience. But here's the rub.

Making video content in any form takes work. I've found it takes more work than many other forms of communication. Even though I'm a "get it in one take" type of person when recording, one take can mean 5 or 6 separate tries to hit everything the way I want to. If I get jammed up trying to get whatever is in my head out, I must start putting up a piece of paper with an outline. And when things get rough, I must take a pause and write out a script. All this activity could result in an hour or two to get that 2- or 3-minute piece of video content just right, or at least good enough.

This leads to the second rub: if the friction of the creative process isn't challenging enough, I also have a day job.   I have yard work. The dog needs to be walked. The car needs to get in for an oil change. So along comes the opportunity to exercise that "maximum flexibility" muscle. To finish just that one piece, sometimes I must get up at 5:30 a.m. to complete it so I can load other things on the plate later in the day. Alternatively, sometimes it is 9:30 p.m. when the camera rolls, which is awful for me because I'm a morning person and prefer to be in bed early most days.

There is a hard line between doing what we want and doing what we need to do. Real progress is realized when we do what we need to do.

Before I entered the world of micro-fame, I mentored many young and talented people. I still do. A young man who knew one of my close friends asked me if I could have a coffee with him and discuss how to be successful in his career. I like coffee and helping people, so a sit-down was easy to coordinate.

At the beginning of our conversation, the young man asked me how I had reached the senior executive level in the corporate world.

"I spent a lot of time watching and listening to what other leaders do. I was in a bit of a rut with my career when I came across a news story about Jamie Dimon. Jamie said he wakes up early and reads several newspapers and news sources daily. So, I evaluated my effort and realized I wasn't maximizing my learning, preparation, and focus opportunities. I changed my routine. I get up around 5:30 a.m. I open my work email, and I open several media outlets that I follow. I soak up about an hour's worth of stuff and then try to get a workout. Then I get myself together and dig into the work tasks for the day, usually by no later than 8:00 a.m."

The young man looked at me and laughed. "Man, there is no way I could get up that early. I love my sleep too much."

I looked at him and said, "Then there's no good advice I can give you. If you can't be flexible enough to change your routine to one that improves your chances of success, nothing I can share with you will help."

That might seem harsh, but it isn't. Part of being a good mentor is being honest and blunt with those you mentor. On more than one occasion, my best personal mentors have shared things that hurt my feelings because they were true, and I wasn't exercising the correct amount of self-awareness to recognize them myself.

The young man is fine and doing well. I'm happy to say I didn't crush his dreams.

Maximum flexibility is mandatory in your career aspirations to be a known and recognized voice in your expertise. However, it can also be exhausting and expensive.

Chris Roberts, who I have mentioned before, is an exceptionally well-known cybersecurity expert and a great human being. I know this because we both own Great Danes and Great Danes only hang out with great humans. That's not a boast. My Great Dane loves to hang out with my wife, not me.

Chris once made a fascinating observation about the costs he incurs annually to be "honored" to speak, present, and participate in events and conferences. That's right, paying out of his pocket for the "honor" of speaking and sharing knowledge with others.

Chris is a micro-famous personality who is always in high demand. People want to hear him and meet him. What he shared in his post doesn't just emphasize the degree of flexibility that may be asked of you; it also highlights what I've said before. Being famous with 12 people isn't about getting rich; it is about sharing knowledge with others.

Chris was the Chief Information Security Officer for a company called Boom. He posted on LinkedIn in 2023, and I'm thankful to share this with his permission.

We'd love YOU to come and speak:

The TRUE cost of speaking at a conference...

Let's start with a few ground rules:

- *These are MY numbers for 2023, most sorted, some still projected*
- *This DOES include carting round the whisky case (and SOME refueling of it)*
- *The rare stipends cover some expenses from places that can't/don't pay*
- *I CHOOSE to do this*
- *Boom pays for nothing, I have the grace of time and that's all I ask for*
- *COVID had one silver lining, the cost of attending, hanging out, and talking at a conference was a whole lot simpler, easier, and less nightmarish. You rolled out of bed, brushed teeth, combed any hair you had/have, and put something on the top half of your body, and sat in front of a camera. There were no travel, hotel, TSA, customs, or conference hall logistics to navigate.*
- *Conversely, no friendly hugs, hallway conversations, sharing of experiences, whisky, or family catch-up.*

Which is why being back on the road is a mixed blessing.

I'm still useless at asking for business class to be covered:
    (Getting old sucks, having diabetes, being tall, and old means I REALLY don't want to be squished in the back of a plane for 4-6-8-10 hours.)

I'm still running imposter syndrome:

(Asking for a stipend or something to cover the time put into building out a deck, let alone time lost to travel etc. is STILL a challenging thing for me to do.)

Rare is the approach made with fully formed ideas AND compensation:
(Feels like an impossible thing for many conferences to offer up front.)

I build mostly unique decks for EACH conference:
(Upside keeps things fresh; downside takes more time, planning, and focus to make sure it's the right thing for the right audience etc.)

This is ALL optional:
(To some degree, we're not in the education world of publish or perish, but we are expected TO be out, talking, leading, helping, guiding, and advancing the industry.)

So, 2023:
32 Conference invites (NOT including podcasts, etc.)
5 Declined (conflicts, or simply TOO much out of pocket)
6 Online
6 Outside of mainland USA
$51,500 total costs (spent AND projected)
$30,000 covered (flight, hotel, etc.), including $12,000 re-invested from stipends
$12,000 in stipends (see above) used to cover other conference expenses
$21,550 out of personal pocket

There you have it, in the clear. This isn't a "job," it's not income by ANY stretch of the imagination, so when I AND others ask if

you can cover some of the costs it's not because we're being an
ass, it's simply that we're spending a lot to help as much as we
can, and anything helps.

Again, it's always optional, but if you want us to come and hang
out, please at least IF you have a budget don't be shy in offering
some of it up. After all this doesn't account for ANY of the time it
takes to build the decks, logistics, meetings, etc.

'all for now

Chris

I know 100 folks just like Chris. People in every area of expertise make sacrifices and choices they'd rather not make. People who also understand that a speaking gig, panel, or interview opportunity will never manifest at a date or time that is convenient to our respective calendars. I know exactly the tolls and taxes that being given the "honor" to speak cost, and I'm forever grateful for someone like Chris itemizing the tangible expenses in such a crystal-clear way. While he hints at some intangibles, they are also worth emphasizing.

Flexibility comes from your willingness to spend time away from your family, friends, pets, and favorite brewery. Flexibility comes in the form of opportunity costs. You could be spending your time on so many other things. You could spend the time you devote to teaching, sharing, learning, and growing your brand, or doing nothing at all. You could be floating in a pool. You could be going to opening day. You could be cutting your grass. You could be caring for or spending time with your children, grandchildren, or parents.

Chris mentions several times that he has chosen this life and that attending these events is optional. Without a doubt, there is a certain amount of self-induced pain when you are famous with 12 people.

But as Chris also highlights, our choice to live this life being famous with 12 people can become quite complicated. People who aren't mindful of the needs and demands that a public speaker on the road constantly must deal with can't process how taxing this life can be. Both emotionally and financially.

Flexibility isn't optional. And flexibility will never be reconciled with "easy." You will make hard choices. You will miss things you prefer not to miss on your personal calendar. You'll sign up for things and then question yourself vigorously about 48 hours before you must be somewhere. "What was I thinking about agreeing to do this?" You will defer maintenance on grass cutting, dog washing, or faucets that need to get fixed. You will most likely pay someone to do it because you know you will never get to it.

Even with all these hurdles, you will still do it. You will show up, honor your commitments, figure it out, and find a way. Flexibility demands it, and the people in your community will appreciate it.

CONTENT, CONTENT, CONTENT

What type of content should I focus on? How much do I need to produce? And should I be using AI to help? In this chapter, we'll explore the strategies for creating impactful content, balancing quality with quantity, and whether AI can be valuable in your content creation process.

You can't be micro-famous unless you create. Creation, for most of us, is content. All kinds of content. And a lot of it.

If you doubt that content creation is necessary for your journey to becoming an internationally recognized expert in something nobody cares about, you're reading tens of thousands of words that took nearly three years to create. This assembly of words was created by an author who has been constantly creating content for several years and writing the book across the same years.

A good friend told me that writing a book is peak content creation. Event organizers and producers have asked me whether I have written a book yet. When would I write a book? How soon could they expect it? There is an unspoken but understood expectation for people who have attained a certain level of micro-fame. You gotta write a book.

I get ahead of myself yet again. Cranking out a book and being an author isn't where the journey starts for anyone. The exception is that you are an author who becomes famous with 12 people because of your books. Then, your journey begins by writing books. Yes, I know that's very circular.

If the emergence of the web has created anything good or great, it has most certainly liberated the control over content by a limited number of publishers, TV networks, newspaper syndicates, and production studios. We live in a world where access to an audience is the easiest it has ever been.

Yes, that means there is a lot of crap content out there. A lot. Like megatons of crap. However, with a limited budget and few barriers to entry, we can all create compelling content in written and recorded media to share with the world. An old laptop, a decent microphone, and an interesting topic are all it takes to start a podcast. Maintaining a podcast over the long haul is a different problem, but getting started is easy.

Our access to a universal distribution network, the World Wide Web, has facilitated the growth of an enormous network of micro-famous people with very specific, unique, and fascinating expertise. You used to have to sign up for paper newsletters at addresses in the backs of guitar magazines or Popular Mechanics or Koi Ponds for Beginners. You used to have to know someone who knew someone to get the skinny on some obscure conference on the Beat Poets and then do a cross-country road trip to get to it.

Unique expertise was localized and spatially isolated. The internet created a highway where all the people with these unique voices and important things to share could get together and grow their knowledge and expertise even further. What's more, the fans, supporters, and critics of those experts could now actively engage with their chosen personalities.

We have the potential to share so much goodness and knowledge! Sure, we waste almost all that potential daily with mindless pursuits on the internet, which provide us with no immediate value other than satisfying our senses or confirming our biases (sorry, was that my outside voice?) without enriching our knowledge base. However, suppose we have the itch to learn and dig deeper into every conceivable specialty, oddity, skill, philosophy, necessity, or urgency in this world. In that case, we can find an expert on the internet.

The internet serves as the distribution channel we never knew we needed—until DARPA fired up those connections and the first bulletin boards popped up. And we've been cranking out content ever since.

There are a lot of decisions to make when it comes to content. I love the precision of the written word, so I do a lot of writing. But what type of writing? Short-form (Twitter/X), medium-form (articles and shorter blog posts, LinkedIn posts), and long-form (books, ebooks) are just a few possibilities. To be clear, not everyone who likes writing is good at all the different varieties of writing.

Some people are exceptional when making a single punchy statement in 100 words or less. Occasionally, I hit a home run in that category. Something a couple of sentences long pops into my head, and I toss it onto business social media. The best part of social media for a content creator (and the worst part) is you have nearly instant feedback. Short forms lend themselves to interaction and exchange with your reader. I love the speedy feedback dynamic of short-form writing. While comments and replies will never be an acceptable proxy for conversation, short-form writing approximates something like a dialogue and can be energizing for a writer.

It can also be exhausting. Because while the written word can be precise, context is challenging to express, and interpretation is always left up to the reader. This is why comment wars can erupt when a writer never intended their observation to be contentious. This reactive component of short-form writing is why many personalities I know shy away from it. If you are guarding or shepherding your personal brand, the volatility of a social media platform and the reaction to your writing can hurt it.

Short-form writing has the advantage of speed, which can be very effective in external communication with your audience. You can be responsive in real-time to events happening around the world. These days, I post about current events in cybersecurity two to three times a week. I probably repost articles or news mentions just as often. However, short-form writing also comes with the risk of inaccuracy or unintentional misfires that can be hard to reel back in.

Short-form writing requires practice. I know, I'm beating a broken drum. I keep saying practice, practice, practice. That is precisely why this book is called a career guide, not a magic trick. There is no success on this journey without practice and repetition. The great thing about short-form writing is you can get a lot of practice doing it. The short-form medium is a volume-based business. If you are reasonably good at pithy observations and statements on short-form digital platforms, you can get even better by frequently posting. Phrasing and word choice improve as you search for the right combination to illuminate an important idea or issue.

Medium-form writing shifts your energy and focus into more planning and thinking. Medium-form writing is rarely spontaneous, but it can be. In the chapter on public speaking, I share a piece I wrote about finding your muse. While sitting on my patio one night, I wrote that piece in one inspired burst. It took a couple of hours, but it was very spontaneous. My medium-format writing is home on platforms like LinkedIn but not on Twitter/X, Telegram, or Mastodon. Quick hit writing on those platforms is typically focused on driving home a single point or notion. Medium-format writing usually expands on a single point or covers multiple angles associated with a topic.

You probably aren't creating an outline for a medium-format written piece, but you will write and rewrite sentences on your keyboard or in your brain until you find the right combination. Blog posts and articles in the 800-to-1200-word range also fit nicely in this medium-format writing category. When I first begin researching a topic covered by an expert, I usually seek their medium format work. The quality of a person's expertise and experience begins to manifest in this format, where the short form allows for little visibility into that quality. I think the broader market tends to doubt the credibility and authenticity of a supposed expert if all they do is create short-format written content.

Long-format writing is rarely easy for anyone. Writing a book or even a short ebook takes time. Lots of time. And planning. And discipline. It is also the least interactive of any written format. Your book isn't open for comments. Your book might get a review on Amazon, but it isn't the same as the bidirectional exchange of online social and business media platforms.

The long format isn't just an investment of time. It is an investment of huge amounts of personal emotion. I wrote an entire section on a topic for this book, and then, poof, it was gone. To this day, I don't know what happened, but the couple thousand words I typed were gone when I reopened my laptop the next day. It was a loss that I grieved. I was angry. I was sad. I don't think I've ever felt bad about a Tweet of mine getting deleted.

Since it has taken me over two and a half years to write this book, I am not the authority you should look to on how to write a book. My friends who have successfully published exposed me to many different approaches. Some are outline people. Some are streams of consciousness people. Some are weekend-only writers. Some are I-write-everyday-at-7-am-for-an-hour writers. Some are writers in spirit only who never get the book written. Regarding the long form, I have no great wisdom for you. The people who influenced me to get this book finished always had the most straightforward and clearest advice on the matter.

Just write.

It is advice that has truly worked for me. I kept trying to tell myself I was a "burst" writer and would write many words when the inspiration struck me. However, those moments of inspiration are usually too few and far between, and life has a way of making those bursts arrive at precisely the wrong time. Those moments have an uncanny tendency to arrive when you have nothing to write with on hand. They come when you are out for the evening with friends. They always manage to show up when the toilet breaks, and you must fix it.

I began to carry my personal laptop with me on my business trips. Even though the extra weight was a pain, it reminded me that I needed to pull that laptop out and write when I had no business obligations. Just that simple step took me from 20,000 words in a year to the completed book you have now in 6 months. It worked for me.

It may not work for you. But again, you don't have to write a book to be micro-famous.

Queue the ominous techno music with the heavy bass drum track.

Should I or shouldn't I use AI?

AI is another topic that I am frequently asked to comment on. I won't dive into my thoughts, concerns, or hopes about AI as a part of this section of the book other than to address it in the context of social media and content creation. I'm writing this book at a time when AI-related companies are starting at the pace of hundreds, if not thousands, per month. The hype cycle is in full swing, from video creation to blog posts and every medium in between. Regarding content creation, almost everyone has that single question in mind.

The answer directly ties to essential concepts I've already mentioned, such as authenticity. The answer also depends on your understanding of how AI works and what it can and cannot do. When it comes to authenticity, it is important to figure out whether AI will generate any type of content in a way that is aligned with your voice, tone, and interests. Remember that your audience determines whether your material is authentic and true to you or not. You might love leveraging a tool like Runway to turn all your short-form videos into a cartoon-style output. However, if your audience isn't enthralled with that output because it is inconsistent with what they've come to expect from you, your audience will wander off to whatever inspires them next.

The authenticity problem leads right to the operational problem: Do you understand how AI works and what it can and cannot accomplish? AI will not and cannot spontaneously manifest material for you. It can produce videos, images, novels, blog posts, social media musings, and a host of other content types, but ultimately, the kernel of the idea or notion that fuels AI comes from your brain.

This is a good thing. You can train AI to generate outputs representing your tone, thoughts, or mannerisms. AI will undoubtedly get even better at this capability over time, but I doubt that the outputs will ever get better than a close approximation of your tone, thoughts, and mannerisms, which means that AI isn't a "set it and forget it" tool. You must still put in the work to review, edit, and finalize the content created by AI.

Putting in that work is an effort you must consider when using AI tools. There is no "easy" button for content creation or social media engagement. AI does represent an "easier" button, but you must be diligent about ensuring that what AI tools spit out is accurate (and accuracy is a problem now). You must ensure that it represents your voice, tone, and style and that the kernel of the idea is yours, not a plagiarized thought or concept.

There is also the investment in time you must include to become a decent user of AI tools. You must become adept at various AI skills, from prompts to editing to modifying and perfecting. A great example is a tool like Jasper. While it is a powerful tool that can accelerate any written content you would like to produce, it also requires substantial learning. Jasper classes are available through several different venues, but now you are also adding cost to an already pricey subscription for the tool itself.

Cost is a consideration you cannot escape regarding AI. None of the AI tools available that are up to creating the type of content you need are free. Some AI tools have base subscriptions that are spendy. Suppose you begin to buckle together a set of tools for video, podcast, image creation, blog writing, social media posting, and any other strategies that fit your program. Those costs will add to a hefty monthly or annual bill.

Don't allow cost to be a prohibitor from using these technologies if they net to a return on value to you. It is equally important that you are realistic about what the value return will be. For example, it takes you 100 or 200 hours to master any of these tools. That is 100 or 200 hours, and you mentally need to account for how you could have used that time to create whatever you rely on AI to output. The payback period may be quite a bit longer than you think it is.

Producing content is an investment in your personal brand. You won't find many free methods, tools, or outlets. Even when they are free, "free" comes with some cost. There could be limitations on how many emails, how much digital storage, how frequently posts can be made, or any other threshold restrictions that minimize the impact you can generate with those tools. In truth, nothing of value is ever free. The hours upon hours expended in learning the tech, or the lack of accessible audiences, aren't the same as a monthly bill from a service provider. Nevertheless, these are still costs.

Content creation starts organically for almost all of us. As you move into the famous with 12 people part of your career, you have strategic and tactical decisions. Figure out where you fit from a format perspective and then commit a strategy to paper. Don't go sign up for three different video creation platforms. Use your network and contacts to pinpoint the solution that meets most of your strategic needs. The same goes for your social media platform choice for content delivery. Do your homework. Don't assume that one person's success on one channel guarantees you the same success.

The content game is essential. Don't let it "just happen" as you develop your personal and professional brands. Production is challenging, particularly as your brands grow. Finding time to produce content will become problematic. But as demanding as the production part can be, becoming a knowledgeable master of distribution is what matters. Content that doesn't get delivered to the right audience and the right eyes is wasted time, effort, and energy.

Now, let's look at content and distribution channels you don't control directly. For many people, popular media is the pinnacle of achievement when it comes to being micro-famous. However, others control access to popular media and what eventually gets broadcast or posted in print. Understanding how their world works and what they find compelling enough to quote you about is crucial to getting your first or four-hundredth media placement.

LOOK MA, I'M ON TV! AND IN THE NEWSPAPER!

How do I land a spot on TV? Is there a formula for getting my quotes featured in the media? And what types of media outlets should I target? In this chapter, we'll break down the strategies for gaining media coverage, explore the different types of outlets, and reveal how to position yourself as a go-to expert for the media.

Getting on TV, podcasts, online media networks, or having your quotes picked up in print media may not be interesting to you. For those of you who find this opportunity intriguing, there is a lot of knowledge and information worth sharing on how to do it. Even if these modes of media are not on your radar yet, you never know when you might be unexpectedly called upon to give an interview.

Tips, tricks, traps, and pitfalls are associated with getting into any media-related channels. Getting a "pick-up" can be a huge accelerator and amplifier of your personal and professional brand, although it isn't guaranteed. There are a lot of misconceptions about how powerful these interviews, conversations, and quotes are. Some of these misconceptions are tied to a misalignment of expectations on our part, and some are the functional realities associated with the massive quantity of good and bad content that fills our ears, eyes, and inboxes daily. The world of market-facing content is more than just what you see on television.

TV isn't just TV these days. I was a kid when color TV was still reserved for fancy families, and there were only three primary networks to choose from. Most of us had black and white TVs with a coat hanger antenna. When the knobs inevitably broke, we may have even used a pair of pliers to change the channels. Thankfully, in that era of restricted content availability, we had UHF, which had all the glorious and goofy local channels and programming we could ever want.　There were no more than two or three local channels, and they were no further than 40 miles away from our television sets. Today? There are an infinite number of channels. Only a small percentage are tied to network broadcasting juggernauts like CBS, NBC, ABC, Bloomberg, CNN, ESPN, and Fox.

The internet has created an explosion in video-based content. Anyone can be a network because the distribution problem of analog-based wavelengths has been defeated. As with all things on the internet, this is yet another part of the online world that is both a blessing and a curse. The liberation and democratization of video content is fantastic, but it also means that a lot of that content is awful or should never see the light of day. Great news, though! It's even easier to change the internet channel than in the old days. And you don't even need a pair of pliers!

Diving into the process of getting invited to be a part of agency-based content creation is a discussion that breaks down into two distinct components. First, how do you even get invited to the dance? To be perfectly blunt, this is the hardest part of the entire process. There aren't "open calls for responses" floating around in the atmosphere on conference pages looking for speakers and panelists. There aren't marketplaces where you can easily pitch your background and expertise like speakers' bureaus. Almost none of us have personal public relations professionals actively digging for opportunities for us. We don't have journalist buddies who are just salivating for the chance to use our specific knowledge for a pending story. Cracking the egg of any level of media exposure feels like an impossible dream for most people.   I'm not going to deny that it can be very challenging. But growing your career and brand in that direction is worth the effort.

The second challenge to consider is how you dance after you get invited. There are a lot of ways that you can interact with the media, interviewers, and hosts. There are several correct ways to do it and a whole list of wrong ways. The benefit of doing it the right way is it leads to even more opportunities. Once you've established yourself as an engaging personality in your market or field, getting more chances to be interviewed or asked for quotes becomes a self-perpetuating machine. My goal is to share the right dance moves with you so that after you score that first date, you just keep boogying.

There is no magic formula or spell to getting your first call for a podcast, TV interview, or guest spot. I wish I could tell you that all you need to do is (insert something here), and "poof!" you end up in a chair answering questions. Nothing in the media and entertainment world works that way, whether it is the nightly news or a gal in California with a kick-ass podcast subscribed to by tens of thousands. There are ways to make it happen that are free, there are ways that cost money, and there are ways that are just pure serendipity because luck isn't part of the path to micro-fame. I intend to cover a variety of ways that can get you to the desired outcome, but it won't be an exhaustive list. There may be opportunities and avenues I haven't seen or personally experienced. But if you are attentive to the events, activities, and conversations around you that align with your interests and expertise, you'll recognize the possibility when it manifests.

Let's start with the easiest route first.

If you already have an established persona in your area of knowledge, you are probably circulating with people who have similar passions. This is a broad assumption because maybe you aren't currently interacting with people who are inspired or fascinated by that subject. I doubt it because those people would be identifying or declaring you an expert, a guru, or a thought leader in the first place. But it is possible.

If this is the case, I need you to pause reading this chapter and get to work on that first. Your community is your fuel supply, distribution center, and talent agency. Even though I'm about to recommend the easiest approach, it can also become the most productive in the grand scheme of things. The power of your community and those who follow you can generate opportunities more than an entire army of public relations specialists, booking agents, and journalists.

If you have that extended community of support to tap into, start exploring. Seek out people hosting podcasts and video segments about your focus area. Heck, you may already be tapped into them and leveraging their platforms. But, then again, maybe you are not. The enjoyable thing about niche or narrow areas of expertise is that there are usually established forums you can tap into. I love podcasts. I think they are the best example of the kind of positive force that the internet can be. Podcasts consist of thousands of people talking about, reporting on, and sharing ideas, thoughts, and observations on a vast myriad of topics. Whether the people in your community are shooting short video segments or sitting down for 30-minute dissections of some fascinating subject, simply asking to join can be the perfect entry point into this part of your career growth.

Podcasts and getting on them frequently generate questions. Should I have a podcast, too? Should being on a friend, colleague, or follower's podcast require me to ask them to be on mine? Before I get to the edge of the deep, dark rabbit hole of podcast creation, production, and promotion, I'll share my experience in this space.

I don't have a podcast, or at least I don't at the time I'm writing this book. Realistically, I will probably start a podcast that complements this book. I would love to talk to hundreds of people who are famous with a different set of 12 people than I am. I would also love to introduce those people to other people who might not even know they exist. But as of today, I don't have a podcast. Even without a podcast, I still am on a lot of podcasts. I haven't counted, but I've averaged around a dozen podcasts as a guest each year for a while. Give or take a couple in any given year. So clearly, quid pro quo in the podcast world isn't an absolute necessity. I know many stellar podcast hosts who don't have their own podcasts. They are hosts of company or organization podcasts. And there is probably a good reason for that.

Podcasts take energy, resources, and – well, time. The barrier to entry into the podcast game is almost non-existent. Do you have a computer? Do you have a microphone on that computer, or one attached to it? Do you have access to the Internet? Boom! You're in business. You have everything it takes to be a podcast mogul.

Not really. Just kidding.

While the hurdles and obstacles to starting a podcast are ridiculously low, an old laptop, cheap microphone, and slow internet connection aren't going to launch you into the stratospheric heights of a highly subscribed-to podcast. There are exponentially more low-quality and barely listened-to podcasts than successful ones. Even among successful podcasts, those that generate income for their creators are probably a fraction of that total. My friends who are podcasters, specifically those who do it well, invest themselves in them fully.

Not just from a monetary perspective, but they are fully invested in the development and growth of their brand. Sounds familiar, right? Imagine that! Podcasters can be micro-famous too! A whole lot of them are. A friend of mine produces the longest-running cybersecurity podcast on the market. Raf Los is the host and creator of "Down the Security Rabbit Hole." I know, right now, you realize that I said earlier that I would wait before taking you down the rabbit hole. Pretty slick, right?

Raf's podcast has made him one of the most well-known voices in cybersecurity. His isn't the voice that drops media quotes or sits across from an interviewer, but the voice that asks the questions and digs into the thorny issues this industry faces. From the biggest breaches to the most specific skills in cybersecurity, Raf probably has an episode about it.

Raf doesn't produce a low-quality podcast. He has the tools, the talent, and the components necessary to deliver a great recording that people want to listen to. He has sponsors. He also has a keen ear for the details, asking insightful and sometimes piercing questions about his industry. Even though he has this long-running episodic podcast, which generates off-setting revenue for his equipment and hosting costs, Raf is still a practitioner in the field. Podcasting hasn't replaced his day job. Neither has his day job reduced his passion for creating great content.

Being a guest on a podcast doesn't require you to have a podcast. If you want to create a podcast or already have one, that's cool. Among the long list of topics I'm not an expert on in this book, podcasting is again in that count. If it interests you, get after it. There are a lot of resources out there you can tap into to learn and develop your podcast Jones.

Podcasts aren't just limited to those created by friends and family. There are paid podcast opportunities as well. By paid, I don't mean you get paid. Some wildly successful podcasts charge fees for guests to appear. It might sound a bit off-putting if you've never heard of this. Why would I have to pay to be on someone's podcast or video content? It is a matter of simple economics. Some podcasters are very successful and have mastered their efforts in monetization. They don't just host headline sponsors that underwrite their show costs.

Their podcasts command a large enough audience to guarantee broad exposure for guests or their companies. This podcast type doesn't generally show up in your inbox as an invite one day. These productions and creators typically interact with public relations firms and other agencies to secure talent. And they are very good at recognizing existing and up-and-coming micro-famous people. When I was approached for these types of engagements, the host or their staff did a lot of homework about my previous appearances. This suggests, then, an exchange of value. The podcaster has a huge audience that is precisely the kind of population that you want to reach. The podcaster also needs the talent to keep that audience inspired and grow their audience.

I love the podcast medium. It is a content channel that you never grow out of. It is the perfect " baby step" entry point for people to introduce themselves to the mechanics of being interviewed and sharing their knowledge. You don't have to leave the podcast orbit as your reputation and brand grow. You can participate in small and large podcasts, move into paid podcasts, develop your podcast, or try out new talk tracks on podcasts. From a few followers to a subject matter dynasty, podcasts cover all the levels, stages, and ages of your career growth.

The next media category is where the journey goes from a solo act to a team event. I don't know many well-known experts in any field who are called on by television networks, media groups, content agencies, or conferences simply because of who they are. There are exceptions to this rule, but the complexities of media production make them rare. The blistering timelines demanded of media organizations to get the news on the wire the fastest and the lack of everyday visibility of most micro-famous people contribute to these complexities.

In every big market vertical, specialty content and media organizations exist. Banking, law, fashion, cybersecurity, automobile manufacturing, car racing, extreme sports, sporting goods—you name the industry, and many publications, online broadcasts, digital print outlets, and insider content creators exist.

The next level is broadcast media of almost every type. You might think that a local television station is easier to get on than a national or global broadcast network. Surprisingly, the effort to get invited to either isn't any different. Sometimes, local broadcasts can be even harder because the access pathways to break into them are tightly guarded within that city or metropolitan area. People often wrongly believe that a local broadcast opportunity is "lesser than" a national broadcast opportunity. An interview or commentary in a major market like San Francisco, New York, Los Angeles, or Boston can be a much bigger "get" than a seven-second quote on a national or global broadcast.

The ultimate level is being a regular commentator or "expert" for one or all the national and global broadcast networks. While I haven't reached this level yet, I know some people who have. When you get there, you're standing on the great dividing line between micro-famous and truly famous. Or at least broadly famous. Only at this level do you become the person that people call without the intervention and participation of many other players.

But let's revisit who and what those players are and start from the specialty end of the media funnel.

Industry-related content outlets are the land of milk and honey for the micro-famous. These media and content creators focus specifically on the areas we work in as experts. Whether quilting, robots, drones, or cocktail crafting, many companies focus their attention and energy on informing the interested public, consumers, and practitioners. Consumers of their media include buyers, followers, participants, hobbyists, professionals, and those seeking professional growth. The distribution power of the internet has taken what was once very specific and unique specialties, sub-specialties, and niche knowledge domains and given them wings. Or, if you prefer, it has given them bandwidth.

Whatever your area of effort is tied to, you've got access to various online avenues. If you are just starting your journey to becoming famous with 12 people, expand your research to find media outlets that tie directly and indirectly to your passions. Also, look for these opportunities outside of your community bubble. By that, I mean research globally. There are great media channels all over the world.

Pitch to as many of them as you can. If you've already grown a healthy audience, you are probably aware of many (if not most) of these outlets. Don't limit your horizons.

Indirect or adjacent domains are also ripe grounds for planting quotes or writing guest blogs or articles. In my case, cybersecurity is a topic of great interest outside the cybersecurity community. Consumer protection, banking, insurance, healthcare, national infrastructure, government, and legal professional communities are all generally interested in digital security. Finding content publishers who want cybersecurity commentary that is relevant to their audience is easy. This approach expands your reputation, credibility, and impact beyond your community.

This raises a point about understanding the audience you are speaking to outside of your focused experience. As you knock on the virtual doors associated with these adjacent media channels, you must be conscious of the expectations awaiting you once they open. You will be expected to phrase your knowledge, advice, and recommendations so your community will understand. Every part of our life is exposed to the truth that each component has a different language or taxonomy. Doctors and nurses don't understand security in healthcare if it isn't directly tied to the things that are important to them and how they provide that healthcare to others. Speaking or writing in a language that approximates the problems and solutions in their world is an expected requirement on our part.

Doctors and nurses shouldn't have to learn digital security to understand what we are saying. Usually, this means we must share our knowledge in the form of use cases that we jointly understand. For doctors and nurses, I frequently share insights about the problems of managing digital assets in a hospital, surgery suite, or maternity ward. How do you log into a device securely when you've scrubbed up and gloved up and can't touch a keyboard or device without having to re-do the entire sterilization effort? That's an example of an adjacency with digital security that also happens to be a tricky real-world problem in healthcare.

Once you start pushing into those other areas where your knowledge can be helpful, don't forget the power of storytelling we've discussed. A three or four-sentence quote can be a whole story that resonates with people who wouldn't otherwise know anything about what your industry does to help theirs. Before you say, "You can't tell a story in three or four sentences," I'll just say one word. Haiku. The art of telling a compelling story in only a few short sentences or even with a handful of words is as old as humanity. There are global competitions for events like "6 Word Science Fiction." Words are incredibly powerful. Stories are epically powerful. Understanding the function of the economy of words results in more media pickups in every type of content. Later in this chapter, I will share some important information about how appreciation for the economy of words isn't just necessary and how that appreciation can amplify your results.

I mentioned that media engagement at this level and beyond is a team event. When you are a solo act, researching and directly connecting with the media channels in your field is a must. Building networking relationships with these channels' reporters, analysts, bloggers, and producers is also mandatory. But this direct approach comes with no guarantee of success. Even in the smallest of specific knowledge domains, there can be a lot of noise.

The people who run these channels are constantly researching and digging into the internet for information they can use. They may have a specific stable of experts they are comfortable working with on stories. They may have paid media arrangements with companies that give them a better shot at scoring an invitation, quote, interview, or submitted article. They probably don't have time to confirm your credibility or experience, meaning you must be able to quickly direct them to a source that expedites that effort for them, like a website URL that is your name and serves as an aggregation point for all your other created materials.

Sometimes, most of the time, it takes a team. The "team" I'm talking about is public relations and marketing specialists. Companies of every size either have them or have access to them. You can even contract a PR firm for yourself, although that is a step that happens after you've grown your brand and visibility to the level where you can afford it. It's not cheap.

During my first few weeks in a public-facing role, I was introduced to my company's internal PR and communications leader and our external public relations firm. I didn't know what to expect, as I had not yet interacted with a PR function in the corporate world. Except, of course, on the rare occasion when we had a charity event or announcement, and I was part of a larger group of executives trotted out for the photo ops and the crafted quotes. By well crafted, I mean that there was no freestyling" at these types of events. PR and media handlers ensured we all stayed true to a script and hit the key points and topics we were prepped for.

Because I had access to great PR specialists on these occasions, I learned quickly how it all worked. I did have another advantage, though, one that I hadn't shared with anyone on the executive team before I got hired. I am one of the few people in cybersecurity who also has been an elected official. My elected office was non-partisan by law, so no one needs to worry about political ideologies or leanings on my part. I was an elected school board member for the 9th largest school district in the State of Ohio. Before that position, I had run for partisan elected office twice. I was destroyed in both elections, but those campaigns taught me incredible lessons about the media and how to interact with them. If nothing else, it taught me that I didn't want to run for office in a partisan election ever again.

I started like a lot of people do when they run for office, as a political novice. I thought I could convince people to vote for me because I laid out very reasoned, researched, and well-thought-out positions for every possible thing the voters would be interested in. I thought trying to be smart would guarantee a win in an election field where, frankly, the opponent wasn't the brightest bulb in the box. And boy, oh boy, was I wrong.

As I said, I got destroyed in two different elections. After my first election failure, I evaluated what I had done wrong and what I needed to change. I had no specific plans to run for office again, but serendipity came calling. So, I ran for a county office a few years later. I didn't have the energy or the motivation to try to be clever that round. The humbling experience of the previous election always sat on my shoulder like a parrot squawking, "You're not as smart as you think you are." I realized voters don't want the owner's manual version of your political beliefs. They want sound bites to reassure them that you care about and are genuinely interested in the issues that are important to them.

Sound bites. If you learn nothing else from this career guide on being a micro-famous personality in your expertise, sound bites can and will make your efforts easier. This doesn't just apply to being famous with 12 people. Running for elected office taught me the importance of word economy.

I've said it multiple times in this book. I'm a talker. A whole lot of a talker. So, the economy of words was foreign and uncomfortable to me. How can you deliver a message about a complicated topic or challenging issue in a few words? I mean, societal problems are complex. Cybersecurity problems are complex. Mastering things like trap shooting, gymnastics, or the piano requires you to move from the simple and fundamental to the complicated and advanced. There is so much to talk or write about and so many nuances and considerations to communicate. While this may be true, none of it matters to a listener, an audience, a reader, or a voter. What matters is the concise abstraction of something complicated into stories, metaphors, and sound bites that make those matters clear and relatable.

Being a talker isn't the only challenge or most significant barrier in mastering word economy. I'm living proof that a loquacious bloviator can be taught to speak and write in a powerful short form that gets results. The natural barrier to being a successful word economist is ego. We want to sound smart; we want to be smart, and we want others to believe we are smart. Our ego drives us to prove our smartness, prowess, strength, convictions, and beliefs. Ego forces us to talk when we should probably listen. Ego requires us to fill the silence void and keeps us from being concise.

No matter how smart we are, our anterior cingulate cortex and fronto-insular cortex (or whatever other part of the brain is speculated to house our ego) take over and get us in trouble. This is why humility is so essential in the communication equation. If you can tame your ego and keep it in check long enough to distill those swirling thoughts into one or two knock-out punch sentences, you will be on your way to getting media pick-ups, quotes, and interview opportunities.

Being an elected official forced me to recognize this dynamic. Becoming a public personality has demanded that I get better every day. Learning firsthand about crafting and delivering sound bites unexpectedly pre-paved my path to success in my famous with 12 people lifestyle. It also reinforced one of the best criticisms I ever received in my corporate executive life.

A boss once told me, "Bird, if someone asks you what time it is, don't tell them how to build a Swiss watch. Just tell them what damn time it is." If there was ever a better aphorism that explained what a sound bite is, I'd never heard it.

Having access to a PR team can be a game changer. PR specialists are constantly digging into the posted and the unposted requests for comments, quotes, or speaking engagements. These media masters build long-lasting relationships with reporters, organizers, event planners, and media networks. The competition between PR firms is also fierce. Their weapons of choice? Personalities who understand how the media and content selection game works, who follow their directions, and who consistently deliver on their requests.

While writing this chapter, I had an opportunity to sit down with a couple of members of my external PR team. We enjoyed coffee and talked about how hard it is for PR teams to get the response and urgency needed to win the battle for media placements and interviews. They shared how senior-level executives, founders, and CEOs don't always appreciate or understand the mechanics of the media world. They typically see responses to inquiries come days after the request, even though replies are needed within hours or minutes. Worse are the responses to immediate demands for a quote or statement by a media outlet. All too often, they receive pages of paragraphs that dive into the reporter's request in excruciating technical details.

If there is a universal "Achilles heel" for smart people, it is the irresistible urge to over-explain.

Winning quotes and interviews from open calls by the media aren't just viciously competitive. It is unforgiving in its urgency. Time won't wait for you to sort out all the intricacies you feel you must express in your head. Reporters won't read paragraph after paragraph of your well-crafted and lengthy manifesto to find the salient, clever, or novel revelations embedded in your reply.

I'm about to share the most important lesson I've learned over several years of being famous with 12 people. Word economics and sound bites are important, but knowing this unwritten rule is the absolute difference-maker when it comes to success in the media.

A good quote fast will always beat the perfect quote that comes in last.

A correlated unwritten rule that we have all probably heard at one time or another is, "Don't let perfect be the enemy of good." The media has neither time nor patience for perfection. While many would argue that this is problematic because the media is constantly forced to simplify complex issues, that argument simply validates a lack of understanding about how the media at every level works. Even with the liberation of the means for distribution within the media world, the game of attracting eyeballs and growing viewers is something close to a blood sport.

While there are more avenues than ever to share information, major media, and social media have an outsized influence on editorial restrictions on the internet. Young or small digital content players are in daily street fights to increase their subscriber count and drive their companies' advertising revenue returns upward. Slow just isn't in the vocabulary of media and content creators.

Sometimes, a reporter or media outlet looks for a longer lead time, usually when building a more in-depth article or conducting investigative journalism. The trick is that you already need to be a known entity to a journalist for these kinds of pieces. You'll build relationships with media players if you are good at meeting deadlines and churning out compelling quotes and content. Earning the right to be a "speed dial" for a reporter or interviewer is a true measure of success. However, it takes time and consistency of delivery to reach this level.

Most of the time, though, the request to respond to a reporter or a media outlet is within hours or by the end of the day. You won't be the only one receiving that request, either. It is being floated to several different personalities through their PR firms. You are in a foot race with everyone else who has received the request. You don't have to be the best runner, but you must be the fastest to the finish. You must shorten the distance to the finish line by focusing on delivering the good instead of the perfect. A good quote, especially a good quote with a memorable sound bite or controversial (but supportable) position, will get you a pickup before the competition has even started working on their response.

At the beginning of this book, I shared how it came to be. An opportunity with my staff caused me to realize that all the components needed to be a recognized personality are teachable. The event that triggered this realization was a rapid response media request. I want to share the formula I shared with them. While it isn't the only approach for responding to media requests, I can tell you that this approach has netted me a success rate that approaches 100%. As many PR experts and media contacts have told me, this batting average is almost unheard of. It is a batting average that I cannot take credit for individually. I get the joy of working with great internal and external PR experts. If they weren't constantly hunting for opportunities,

I wouldn't get any chances to step up to the plate. My job is to be like the lead singer in a rock band. The whole band and our support network of roadies and engineers, lighting specialists, and catering services come together. I get to step up to the microphone when we get our shot. Delivering a good quote fast is like perfectly hitting the opening notes of a song. It honors the entire team.

It's easy to get a fat head when you get a couple of media pickups. But this is a team sport. We just get the privilege of being the voice that delivers the win for the whole team.

The method I've developed to achieve the results I've had over the last several years is a repeatable formula. It isn't the only method. I've met many experts in many fields, and this model has other successful variations. However, the pattern is similar between all these approaches. They all value speed of response, precision in language, and brevity. Notice I didn't say anything about "best." Perfection is the enemy of good when it comes to media responses. This doesn't mean that quality is a non-existent component of your response. Crappy, poorly constructed, and incomplete quotes won't get any pick-ups, ever.

The formula isn't magic. You won't get guaranteed placements with it. You will most likely see your first attempts rejected. However, consistently exercising this or a similar approach will provide the practice and repetition you need for a better final product. Becoming a master quotist takes time, discipline, and practice, practice, practice, just like any other skill.

THE FORMULA

I use what I like to call the 3:2 formula for almost all my rapid media responses. On rare occasions, I may use the 3:3 formula: three sentences, two separate responses, or two paragraphs. 3:3 is simply three sentences and three paragraphs. Let me be clear about this formula. It is a guide, not a hard and fast rule. Sometimes, I might push a given response or paragraph to four sentences. There is rarely ever a time when I exceed four sentences.

This response structure forces brevity, focus, and accuracy on us as writers. The word and response count results in a quote that can be read in approximately 10 seconds. While 10 seconds doesn't seem like a long time, most news pieces will usually only take a reader 3 minutes or less to get through. 20 to 30 seconds worth of quotes fits neatly into the time dimensions of most online stories. The other benefit of a 10-second read is that the reporter or interviewer who has requested it can read your concise quote quickly, upping your chances of being "good and first."

The formula isn't just about sentence count and paragraph length, though. What you do with the three or four sentences and the two paragraphs delivers the results. When you build your responses, each sentence in a paragraph should be able to stand alone and still be a good or viable response to the question. This results in not just two responses but six responses across two paragraphs. The reporter can choose between those sentences to create an entirely different quote. This may sound a bit complicated, but it isn't.

This response formula gets easier with practice. The more you force yourself to follow this formula, the faster you will become. The formula also forces you to be precise in answering the proposed question. While perfection is the enemy of good, precision is a necessity when it comes to rapid responses. You can't wander in your response if you limit yourself to 3 sentences.

The first sentence of any response should attempt to restate the question the journalist or content creator asked. This can be tricky if the requester asks a long, rambling question. In that case, you may have to distill the question to its simplest level. Typically, even a short nod to the original question will prove to the requester that you are focused and know exactly what you are responding to.

I make my first quote the pair's most novel, controversial, or contrarian. Surprising the requester with an unexpected response will differentiate you from the others responding. While the requester might not run with that first quote, a unique take will motivate them to read through the second and the third. Journalists are never looking for a generic response they can get from anyone. It is your responsibility to come up with something different and catchy. This doesn't mean being controversial or contrarian just for the sake of shock value. Suppose you have a strong, evidence-supported opinion or an equally strong and supported belief that the people in your area of expertise are looking at a problem incorrectly. In that case, these are the moments to get that out into the open.

I like to call this approach "saying the quiet parts out loud." In cybersecurity, there are a lot of people who believe the entire industry is doing things the wrong way. Our results clearly show that we aren't delivering security improvements to the digital world. They further show that business leaders still refuse to accept the responsibility necessary for better performance for their customers, stakeholders, and users. The problem, then, is that all these people who share those same beliefs either can't (or won't) say it out loud. If they rock the boat, they may feel they lack the platform to share their observations or have legitimate concerns about their employment or longer-term career impacts.

This type of problem doesn't just exist in my field. It exists in every field, every hobby, and every industry. Progress, evolution, and growth seem logical and desirable paths for our species. Yet the difficult truth is that progress, evolution, and growth threaten the status quo. It takes years, decades, and sometimes even centuries for disruptors, cynics, innovators, and thinkers to break through the thick walls of "this is how it has always been" or "that's just how we do things." Whether it is cell phones and smartphones, agriculture, cancer research, or artificial intelligence, advances in those fields always come with an initial resistance to change. Often, they are met with outright skepticism and criticism.

Change is difficult for almost all human beings. Resistance is elevated when that change comes with the perceived threat of eliminating my job, reducing my budget, forcing me to buy new tech, or reorganizing my company. You can understand why change is actively blocked or impeded by the people or powers with the largest vested interest in things staying exactly the way they are.

Every start-up company knows this truth in bold, vivid, and painful detail. It doesn't matter what product it is; you are either introducing a new way of solving an old problem or rethinking it and its resolution altogether. Both approaches directly threaten the companies that have already grown and gained revenue. Both approaches run headlong into consumers, experts, communities, and companies already invested in the old tech, old ways, and old trends. The voices, leaders, entrepreneurs, and thinkers who call for change or build that better mousetrap may collect hundreds or thousands of supporters, followers, and believers in their cause or ideas. None of that changes the truth that human beings hate change. Human beings inside corporations hate change unless it provides an immediate and positive revenue increase.

Saying the quiet parts out loud is empowering for people who feel they have no voice or influence, but it is threatening to the maintainers of the status quo. Being the representative for change comes with this double-edged sword. Having this knowledge can be helpful. You will often need to make a personal judgment call on how far to push the envelope. In some settings, hinting about invoking change is more powerful than demanding it. This applies to speaking, writing, and providing quotes or observations. Suppose you are asked to give a quote to a publication oriented to the interests of general consumers. In that case, you don't want to open a can of intellectual whoop ass and hammer on the finer details of how change must happen. A consumer audience is too broad and diverse of a population to embrace your call for change within your community of expertise.

An audience of your peers and a room full of forward thinkers would be an audience where details, vision, and disruption might be the right recipe. It boils down to situational awareness.

Also worth noting is that situational awareness is a crucial component of achieving success in the media. The formula I shared might be helpful for you and yield similar results. But a lack of situational awareness will doom you to a one-and-done batting average. Frankly, situational awareness is the key to many things beyond media, speaking, and presenting. The subject itself is worth a book or ten.

Interviews are the type of media-facing transactions that require the most situational awareness. When you work with a PR firm, you'll be briefed on who you are talking to and an overview of their interests. A full briefing will give you background on the interviewer or journalist and links to other pieces, segments, or stories they've published. You must read it all, dive into every link, and understand the perspective and orientation that the interviewer has coming into the discussion. Walking (or Zooming) into an interview without having done the preparation work to gain insight and situational awareness is like swan diving into a pool filled with bear traps. Interviewers can immediately recognize an unprepared interviewee. Like a job interview, if the journalist you talked to says thanks for all the information ten minutes into a thirty-minute appointment, you did not get the job.

Situational awareness doesn't end with interview preparation, though. If you are working for a company, many media contacts will insist that you don't turn your opportunity into a commercial for your solution, service, or offering. It is terrible form if you do. If you do not have the presence of mind to keep yourself from blathering on about how cool your (insert cool stuff here) is, you'll never get another interview opportunity again.

There are exceptions to the no-sales-pitch rule. If you are talking to analysts covering your specific industry, they may want a complete understanding of what your company or organization offers. But these situations aren't quite like media or content interviews.

Hopefully, the formula I shared is beneficial. I can't guarantee it will be, but I have experienced consistent success using it for several years. I hope you experience this success, too.

BUT WHAT ABOUT TV?

Getting onto major broadcast media of any kind is the toughest nut to crack in your evolution as a personality. A big reason for this is the undeniable reality stated in the title of this book. You are only famous with 12 people! Broadcast media is almost entirely (but not always) limited to well-known names or people with significant titles, like CEO or founder.

A great example of this dynamic is a show like Mad Money on CNBC, hosted by Jim Cramer. A few years ago, I had the opportunity to interact with Jim to prepare for a segment featuring the CEO and founder of the company where I worked. It was a blur of produc- tion assistants, email messages, and texts circulating among several people at CNBC and my company. My CEO mentioned several times to the production staff that he thought I'd be a great guest on the show.

Guess what? Never happened.

And I understand why. I'm not a CEO. Or a founder. Or an investment analyst. I don't run a venture capital or private equity firm. I'm not a well-known economist or a governor of the Federal Reserve. Sure, many of those different players are probably micro-famous. They also fit the profile of what the viewers of Mad Money expect: important people with important things to say about companies, investments, and the stock market. Cramer's viewers aren't expecting me or anyone else with domain-specific knowledge.

Niche experience or micro-specialization in a specific area of expertise doesn't equal the kind of broad appeal that networks require when a news story breaks, or an industry voice is needed. In business, founders and funders will always be in the highest demand. Experts in any discipline must rely on associating with a highly networked public relations firm. More so, recognition for expertise so specific that the number of known personas to talk with is nearing zero can be chalked up to dumb luck. Okay, maybe dumb serendipity.

Ed Viesturs is an example of an expert voice in the marketplace who occasionally appears on broadcast media and comes from a tiny community of practitioners. About 15 or 20 years ago, I spent a few years learning how to be a mountaineer. Growing up as a "flatlander" in the Midwest, I became fascinated with the idea of reaching the summit of a mountain. It seemed like a natural extension of my rock climbing and hiking interests. In retrospect, and with the benefit of experience on the side of a mountain, I was naïve. Mountain climbing isn't like hiking or rock climbing, and it is not a skill you learn from reading a book or by osmosis.

Technical mountain climbing is intense. At least I was smart enough to recognize that I probably needed quality instruction on the topic. I invested time and money into going to climbing school at the Rainier Mountain Institute (RMI). RMI was started by the Whittaker brothers, twins who would become some of the best-known climbers in the world. Brother Jim would become the first American climber to summit Mt. Everest in 1963. Lou and Jim created a training school in Ashford, Washington that would become what is still the mecca of North American climbing. In the late 70's and early 80's, another flatlander from Rockford, Illinois, would join RMI as a guide, and his name was Ed Viesturs.

Like every hobby I've tried to learn, I dove deeply into American climbing history and culture. So, walking into RMI's storefront and meeting climbers like the Whittakers or Ed Viesturs is not much different than walking into a room filled with movie stars, musicians, or athletes you love and admire. Other than the fact that it is a way smaller community of fans and practitioners. But even among the world's best climbers, Ed Viesturs has notable and unique gifts.

Ed is one of the few people in the world who can climb to the top of peaks over 8,000 meters in height without supplemental oxygen. Ed has climbed every peak over 8,000 meters in height without any supplemental oxygen, making him one of the handful of people in the world with this superhuman trait.

When a significant event happens on a mountaintop in North America or around the world, it doesn't take a lot of effort to understand why the media would be inclined to contact one person to comment on the crisis. And that one person, more times than not, is Ed Viesturs.

The narrower the field of expertise, the smaller the qualified or expert voices population will be. Few expert climbers have summited the world's highest peaks dozens upon dozens of times while never using supplemental oxygen. Of that number, those with media-friendly speaking skills that meet network standards are probably fewer people than you can fit into a Honda Accord. You would probably still have a seat or two left over. Even with his high qualifications, Ed only appears on broadcast media when there is a big news story about a mountain rescue or catastrophic avalanche. Which means his services might go uncalled upon for months or even years.

Being famous with 12 people isn't the most efficient or easiest route to being a regular commentator on broadcast media. Our areas of interest are too small or specific to be in high demand. But there are opportunities if you are flexible, agile, and hungry. I have gotten to provide commentary on media broadcasts with NBC Nightly News, MSNBC, Bloomberg, and a few others.

Why? I've been more than happy to provide consumer-friendly tips, from protecting yourself from scams to securing your credit card during the holiday season.

While those kinds of media moments aren't entirely aligned with my area of focus, being able to provide good, common-sense guidance to consumers is valuable to many media outlets. The flexibility re-quired is taking what you know and making it more generalized and applicable to a broader audience. This requires agility on your part to pivot from the thing you are known for and abstract it up a level for consumption by a larger part of the population. Being personable, approachable, and understandable is more important in the media than being knowledgeable. Being knowledgeable gets you an invita-tion to the dance, but being a relatable personality keeps you getting invited back when it comes to broadcast media.

One pathway to consider is going local. If you live in a metro region with a competitive local network television market, I encourage you to reach out and offer yourself as an experienced resource. You will have to knock on a lot of doors and bump into a lot of dead ends. Local media outlets tend to have very distributed management models, and no convenient door marked "experts, please enter here." You'll find that there are programmers, editors, specialty reporters, freelancers, directors, and producers. Getting to any of these people isn't easy, but it is worth the effort.

Once you associate with a local network, several affiliates within the national network system may pick up something you contribute to. I've had this happen a couple of times. One of my most successful contributions was a media piece I did for a local television station in Boston about the cybersecurity concerns Americans should have because of the invasion of Ukraine by Russia. More than 150 media outlets picked up my little segment within 24 hours. One of those fun moments in my career was when people texted me because they saw my piece on their local news station.

It also was a moment that taught me something inarguable about broadcast media. It is incredibly ephemeral. While it is a crown jewel in the list of accomplishments that any micro-famous person can achieve, your moment on broadcast media is almost instantly forgotten. If you doubt this, I'd ask you to try to recall any specific news story you were exposed to two weeks ago. Do you remember the quoted expert's name? Do you remember what was said? Do you recall why the topic was so important? Probably not.

Broadcast media has this strange dual characteristic of being both necessary and inconsequential simultaneously. It is background noise with occasional flashes of relevance in our day-to-day lives. Because of this weird dynamic, I encourage people not to get fixated

on trying to get a broadcast media assignment. There are so many
other outlets you can access more easily and so many different outlets
that don't expose you to the emotional rollercoaster of the broadcast
realm. If (or when) you get a shot at a broadcast interview, you'll
understand what I mean.

I got the chance to do a segment on Bloomberg for their Closing Bell
segment. I dialed into the teleconference system, and a producer and
an engineer immediately greeted me. We went through a bunch of
instructions. The entire time we conversed, I could hear the Closing
Bell anchors delivering the news on a separate teleconference line.
So, I was trying hard to listen to the instructions I was supposed to
follow, but my ADD was driving me up the wall when I heard the
show happening live. Then, without warning, my teleconference line
merged with the live show's line, and one of the anchors suddenly
asked me a question. I was sweating like I'd already run a 5-minute
mile. The questions started getting fired at me. I stayed focused and
delivered good, concise responses. Three and a half minutes later, it
was over.

I remember telling my wife I needed to lie down and nap. Less than
10 minutes of total effort was enough to blast me emotionally and
physically into exhaustion. With all that intellectual and physiologi-
cal expense comes the realization that nobody even remembers that
I was on Bloomberg's Closing Bell.

I did great; I nailed it.

And no one remembers it.

That's a lot of investment to pour into just one outlet for your voice.
Again, it is worth it, but it shouldn't become an obsession for you. If
serendipity puts the right pieces together and you get the chance, be

awesome. If serendipity doesn't deliver, don't be disheartened. You have many avenues and outlets available to share your voice.

Work with your network, your company resources, your friends, and those serendipitous connections to find ways to get into the public media game. While a media moment is fleeting, and the only people who might remember any specific interview might be your parents or your children, the power of this platform for the expert voice is undeniable. You can reach millions in 30 short seconds. And among those millions, you can positively impact the lives of a few people. It is worth it, even if you are that change for just one person out of those millions.

There's another way, beyond public media, to make your name known. It may not be something that you've ever thought about, but it is advantageous in your efforts to be famous with 12 people. All you must do is claim your name.

WHAT'S IN A NAME?

———————

How can I stand out in the crowded online world? What's the best website URL to strengthen my brand? In this chapter, we'll explore key strategies to boost your web presence and guide you in choosing a powerful URL that aligns with your brand and sets you apart.

———————

There is one tip that I was given a long time ago that is worth sharing and devoting an entire chapter to in this book. And it is all about your name.

As I began forming my thoughts about how to build my personal brand, I had a conversation with a friend with a lot of experience in the mechanics of marketing. He asked me, "Do you own your name?" My initial response was, "Of course I own my name. I'm me!" Except that wasn't the point he was making.

He asked if I owned my name as an internet domain. This was something I had never considered before. Why would I need to own my name? My work was heavily focused on cybersecurity topics and the companies I represented. I hadn't taken a moment to seriously ponder the value of owning my name online.

Several years later, I can boldly declare that it is one of the most important steps you can take, not just for your efforts to be famous with 12 people. From a personal branding perspective, those benefits seem obvious. However, the obvious benefits are only the tip of the proverbial iceberg. Let's talk about getting that URL first because I'm sure some people reading this book have names that may be common and already have been purchased by someone else.

I'll share my story first. When I logged into my hosting service to look up my name, I was bummed to learn that www.richardbird.com had already been snapped up. Nine years ago. When I looked at the registry, I realized that it had been bought by someone looking to sell it. Many companies buy up all kinds of names, slogans, and sayings as potential internet domain names. They sit on them until someone shows up and wants to buy them. There are a lot of individuals who have done the same thing and use these companies as brokers.

There is no specific value assigned to a domain name. You can buy any available name through a hosting company like GoDaddy, Host-Gator, Bluehost, or many other smaller players. Usually, they cost between $9.95 and $14.95 per year. An important safety tip is that you technically don't own your domain name even when you "buy" it. You are renting or leasing it year to year. This distinction is important because it is painful to discover that your domain name has been reclaimed when you fail to pay your annual rent and someone else snaps it up. It happens all the time and can be a costly mistake.

A domain name is one of those things that is worth exactly what someone is willing to pay for it. Complicating matters, though, is that each of these domain names is a unique commodity. There is precisely one of each out there on the interwebs. When it comes to personal names, these name brokers usually will initially ask for a considerable price tag. However, those sellers have a unique commodity problem as well. The market for that name is generally limited to only those with that name, which works in your favor.

A broker bought my name nine years before I tried to buy it. When I requested a quote on how much my name would cost me, a young man emailed me saying he thought he could get the seller to give it up for $6000. Yep, $6000. While you need to own your name as a domain, I can tell you that it wasn't six thousand dollars important to me. When I received the first quote, I became instantly motivated to research. I encourage you to do the same if you are in that situation.

The first thing to note is that the brokerage price for a named domain is a one-time fee. You don't pay that number every year. Once you have secured the lease on that domain, your renewal rate will be the same $9.95 to $14.95 per year that a non-brokered domain would cost you. So, your research needs to focus on every possible angle and way that you can substantiate negotiating that one-time price down as low as possible. I won't say that the companies that broker domain names are dishonest. I will say that they will make every possible excuse to rationalize why they are asking for so much money for that domain, which is why you need data and evidence to make it hard for them to do so.

I immediately searched to see how many other mini-famous Richard Birds were out there. In my situation, there were exactly 3 of us. Focusing on mini-famous people who share your name is essential for two reasons. Reason number one is if you share a name with someone who is mega-famous, that domain name has already been bought and is probably being put to good use. But, if you share a name with other mini-famous people, the market of potential buyers is both finite and known.

Earlier in this book, I discussed two other mini-famous Richard Birds. Richard Bird, the Oxford professor, and Richard Bird, the award-winning actor, are both worthy contenders for the Richard Bird domain name.

Richard Bird was an Oxford professor. Sadly, he passed away in April of 2022. I would have loved to have met him as there is a strange connection between us. He was the Director of the Computing Lab at Lincoln College at Oxford. He was mini-famous because he was the Director of one of higher education's earliest computer programming departments. He was also a key contributor to the Haskell language, the co-creator of the Bird-Meertens Formalism, and a considerable influence on the development of functional programming. Like I've said many times, mini-famous comes in diverse flavors. Professor Bird and I both live in the world of technology. I am confident that Professor Bird would have been sorely disappointed with my lack of math skills.

He was still alive when I was doing my research. However, it was entirely possible, though highly improbable, that this Oxford professor who was more than 25 years my senior might wake up one day and decide, "Man, I need to own my personal name in domain form!" My operating theory was that if Professor Bird hadn't bought his domain name in the early 90s when it would have been much simpler, it would have been a safe bet that he wouldn't snap it up anytime soon.

Richard Bird is an award-winning actor, producer, host, and puppeteer. My second competitor for www.richardbird.com was a serious contender for the crown. RB has been in over 80 films, television episodes, and theater productions. Richard is also someone I'd like to meet in person one day. Part of his back story is that he left the corporate world to pursue acting, meaning that we Birds once again have something in common. We both left the corporate world to pursue other passions. I was in something like 15 theater productions in my teenage years. I'm sure he's way better at acting than I will ever be.

My operating theory about Richard Bird, the actor, was the same as that for Richard Bird, the computer scientist. If neither had bought up the domain name by 2018, when I got the $6000 quote, I felt it was reasonable to believe that there was effectively a total available market of just one buyer: me.

In 2020, Richard Bird, the actor, secured a domain name. His move is a great example of a trick you can try if all your efforts fail to secure your personal name domain. We will revisit that shortly.

Armed with data and evidence, I sent an email back to the person serving as the broker between me and the buyer. Remember I said that the domain brokering business isn't a well-regulated market? On more than one occasion, I've learned that while a broker says they represent an independent seller, they represent their own company. Their company owns the domain name. Domain names don't carry the emotional heft of a piece of art, a vintage car, or a fine watch. The owners of these domain names aren't going to have seller's remorse in the morning. So don't succumb to any pressure tactics when you head to the negotiating table.

I wrote an email and said I would offer $1000 for www.richardbird. com. I didn't want to offer that much. I had already confirmed that there was a market of exactly one qualified buyer for this little gem. Emotionally, I felt the seller should give me the domain for next to nothing. I also knew there was one seller, and one product called richardbird.com, and the seller had held onto and renewed that domain name every year since 2007. Dang it, if I knew I would be famous with 12 people in 2006, I could have saved a lot of money.

I didn't explain my offer, but I thought starting at roughly 15% of the initial asking price was a fair compromise given the "market of one" on each side of the bargaining table. After a few days, the broker responded and said the seller wouldn't take anything less than $2000 for the domain name. The reason? There were other Richard Birds out there.

The seller, however, didn't know what I knew about those Richard Birds. I had already confirmed that neither of those Birds were in play. The seller had no reason to understand the market beyond the existence of humans with the name Richard Bird. Another helpful data point was the seller's decision to counteroffer with an asking price over 60% less than where we started, just on the first try. My opponent flinched in the grand tradition of poker, and I saw his tell. I had everything I needed to win this hand.

I presented my next offer at $1300 and added my detailed rationalization for the number. I explained that there were three Richard Birds with any kind of professional or known personas. One in cybersecurity, one in entertainment, and one in academia. Of those three, one was more than 75 years old and hadn't previously expressed any interest in the domain name in the quarter century before. The other was an actor who could put in an offer, but I doubted that a $6000 tab for the name was his top budget priority. I was a ready and willing buyer right then.

Within a couple of hours, I received the seller's counteroffer, which was $1500. I didn't want to pay $1500, but I knew that haggling over some part of the difference of $200 wasn't worth my time and effort. I returned the acceptance, paid my fee, and confirmed the transfer of www.richardbird.com to my hosting provider within a couple of days.

Securing my name was a win. But it may not be easy if your last name is Smith, Jones, or Miller. The way to combat that problem is just to put on your marketing hat. What domain name would work with that high degree of personal attachment to you, your persona, and your brand? In my situation, I always had a backup plan. The acceptable compromise for me was www.richardwbird.com. Adding my middle initial would have worked, and it would have saved me $1490. I wanted richardbird.com, and I wasn't deterred by $1500 to get it. Not everyone has that economic flexibility, though. If my wife had said I was nuts to pay that much for my name, I would have fallen back to plan B. A middle initial isn't that awkward when you share it with people.

This isn't the only option. I mentioned Richard Bird, the actor, who had taken an interesting approach. In 2020, he purchased the domain name www.rbtheactor.com, which is brilliant. It not only personally identifies him but also crisply identifies his persona. It is short and easy to share.

A very good friend of mine is David Lee. He is micro-famous for a specific type of cybersecurity we have in common: identity. He is famous with 12 people because he is The Identity Jedi. No, seriously, look him up. He's The Identity Jedi. However, DavidLee.com is owned by a country musician and songwriter, David Lee Murphy. His credits are worthy of mention, for sure. He is a platinum-selling artist and has written songs for country stars like Kenny Chesney, Jason Aldean, Luke Bryan, and Eric Church. The problem is that my friend David Lee can't be David Lee. So, he took a clever approach to securing his personal domain, www.IamDavidLee.com. This approach reinforces David's brand as an identity specialist in cyber-security while taking ownership of his name.

Given a choice, don't use any of the .info, .net, or .biz types of options with your name. The reason is the internet world has been con-ditioned to default to .com. It has been the most familiar domain extension for so long that we automatically assume that when you tell me your website URL, I will try it with a .com first, even if I heard you tell me .org. If one of these extensions cleverly ties into your persona, it certainly is an option. For example, if you are known for being a great business consultant, a .biz domain extension might be just the ticket.

After a lengthy dissertation on a personal domain name, we get to the "why" of owning it.

Having a place to showcase your expertise and aggregate information about you, your interviews, your articles, blog posts, podcasts, paint-ings, recordings, or any other item of interest is priceless. I mean it. The simplification that your website brings to your life is worth all the effort and cost to make it happen.

I regularly receive requests to appear on podcasts or webinars. The number one question I receive from PR firms is, "What do you want to talk about?" This question is followed immediately: "What is your presentation or speaking style?" I rarely take any time at all to respond to those inquiries. I just tell people to go to my website, where they will find a broad range of content where I've been a guest, a host, a keynote speaker or had a news media quote. Showing is much better than telling in my line of work. Emotional connection and storytell-ing make my presentation style different from that of most people in cybersecurity. Having an immediately available catalog of some of my content is necessary. For very influential speaking platforms like

TED or SXSW, it is almost mandatory for you to have an accessible aggregation of your past accomplishments.

A personal name domain and website also create a platform for that "brand you" separation from the "brand you on behalf of company x" dynamic I've discussed. Having an independent channel for your personal brand doesn't just create an excellent separation of church and state, so to speak. This means that your name is regularly mentioned in two distinct places from a search engine optimization perspective. This amplification effect is important to expand your reach into a broader population of those interested in your message, experience, and content.

Building, funding, and maintaining a personal name website may not be your thing. Don't think owning your name is worthless in that situation, though. Another powerful benefit of your personal URL is having a very personal email address. Even if you don't take things further by building a website, having the option to give someone a firstname@personaldomain.com email address is all the reason you need to look up your domain and get it locked in. It facilitates the brand separation I mentioned earlier, but it feels empowering when you say, "Oh, just send me an email to rb@richardbird.com."

How you use your personal name domain is up to you. How to effectively maximize your brand, website, message, and content distribution are subjects best left to other books and authors with deep experience. But I'll share one last tip.

If you are the type of personality in your area of expertise that could benefit from trademarking, having a personal website will help you provide a channel to use that trademark. Proving usage is a key part of the trademark process. I only recently learned this as I've gone through the trademark application journey. While $1500 may have been much more than I wanted to spend initially, I know it was well spent in managing my personal brand and the business I have built around it.

THE POPULARITY TAX

———

Things get easier once you become more micro-famous, right? Not exactly. As your visibility grows, so do the number of critics and detractors. In this chapter, we'll discuss the challenges of increased micro-fame, how to handle criticism, and why staying true to your brand is more important than ever.

———

Not everyone is going to love you.

I've already shared the negative social and professional commentary that well-known personalities must contend with publicly. However, there is a mathematical truth that can make this phenomenon even more challenging to navigate. The bigger your brand, the more people who know you, and the more exposure you get, the larger your number of non-supporters will be.

The price of popularity is being unpopular. The taxes you cannot avoid are unhelpful criticism, name-calling, and being the catcher of shade that is thrown. If this entire book were nothing but a rosy picture of how fun it is to become famous with 12 people, I would be doing you a disservice. I would leave you unprepared for the inevitable sharp edges that occasionally cut. Like I said at the beginning of this book, those cuts do and will hurt.

If you purposely or accidentally wander into mini-famous territory, you must have thick skin. There are a lot of critics out there in subjects that range from postage stamp collecting to 15th-century weapons of war to pottery and collecting tiki mugs. I'm not bright enough or experienced enough to be able to provide a rational explanation for why some people feel compelled to be critics. I'm not talking about criticism, which fosters a healthy debate or dialogue. Constructive criticism has a very distinct and helpful role to play in both our personal and professional lives. It is the cruel, useless, and petty criticism that has become the norm in our society today that I'm saying you need to be prepared for when you achieve micro-fame.

I've often said it is far too easy for people to hide behind the quasi-anonymity provided by their digital masks. While many people might use their real names and email addresses to establish their social media presence, many sneak around anonymously by creating false names and accounts. Some of this online presence consists of accounts that aren't even real but are bots intentionally created to sow discord. I don't need to recount any tales of how this behavior manifests on the internet because if you are reading this book, I am sure you are keenly aware of these problematic truths.

You won't face criticism and approbations exclusively on digital channels.

These spiteful criticisms are breaking out of the digital world, and you may even find these behaviors popping up at conferences or events. Don't let this scare you away from the path of helping others.

Your voice is important, and there are ways to help and deflect those who want to harsh your growth just to get in a good verbal jab.

We've already covered the weirdness and the wonderfulness of being seen as an expert. It is worth revisiting that fine line between expert and influencer when you become more known and micro-famous. The criticism I've received the most often is a dismissive "Well yeah, you're just an influencer in this whole new influencer kind of world. Nothing to offer, just trying to be insta-famous." Weirdly, the same people who have no problem following influencers in domains or endeavors that mean little to them have such negative perceptions about influencers or experts in every other part of their lives.

Maybe, just maybe, we've been way too hard on people for being influencers. Sure, there are a lot of influencers who are, for lack of a better term, fluffy. They share lifestyles, advice, or ideas that aren't that important in the grand scheme of things. Judging them on the relative value of their content or messaging might result in your missing the fact that their message and content are valuable to their thousands, tens of thousands, or even millions of followers.

People who fall into the category of "influencers" have their personal brand, too. Quite obviously, the focus of their personal brand is to influence. Hence the name, am I right? Influencers and experts have personal brands aligning with a mission or purpose. It might be tempting to think that an influencer taking a check from a company they don't believe in and promoting that product or cause in your social media feeds or at events is inconsistent, but it isn't. If your brand is all about pushing material goods, ideas, or interests in front of the followers you have, then one more thing added to that mix isn't inconsistent. It is consistent because it is expected.

Again, I'm not offering up any judgment about influencers who engage in these practices. I'm not here to step on anyone's business model or strategy. But I think it emphasizes, once again, that influencers are in the business of making you do, say, or believe something based on their interests. The most common of those personal interests is getting paid. Being famous with 12 people isn't about getting paid. It's about sharing, helping, and learning. Stay focused on that mission.

We must respect the fine line between influencer and expert as we share our beliefs, experiences, and observations. The criticisms we will experience will be seeded in divergent or different beliefs, experiences, and observations within our communities of expertise. An influencer can push a particular energy drink on their social media channels, and if any of their followers don't like that same energy drink, they'll shrug their shoulders and move on. If you offer a controversial observation as an expert, some of your peers and colleagues may not shrug their shoulders. They'll perceive your position as a threat, an affront, or an insult.

You don't have to suffer the slings and arrows. While I want to prepare you for the criticism in your field, remember that you are part of this community that elevated you to the honorific of an expert. Inviting those critics to your table is your best defense and course of action. You are not separate from your community. What drives us is moving our field forward. You can't do it alone. And there is nothing more powerful in advancing the cause than making your critics your allies.

GO FORTH AND CONQUER

———————

You have something important to say.

You have important knowledge to share.

You have a voice that can represent, guide, and support the community, profession, hobby, or interest that you focus on.

I hope that in every chapter of this book, you've found at least one nugget to help you on this journey. I also hope I've helped decode and demystify the "how" of becoming micro-famous. It doesn't just happen on its own. You must consciously decide to steer your career or avocation toward 12 people who will find your views and observations compelling, engaging, and valuable.

I am still and always will be hungry to learn. I don't consider myself an expert on the subject of being mini-famous. I believe I've earned the opportunity to be an experienced navigator for those curious or focused on growing their personal and professional brands. I can tell you for certain that the added joy and the personal and professional growth that has come from my experiences of becoming famous with 12 people have been incredible.

Even if your goals are not inclined toward being a public personality or known quantity in your profession or avocation, I hope this book contains many helpful and valuable tips you can leverage in your growth. You don't have to be the face out front, and you don't have to be the name that everyone knows. Incorporating the powers of storytelling, networking, or growing a personal brand will be valuable additions to your skills, professional and personal tool kit, and career growth.

This book represents an artifact that I hope will lead to the possibility of me being famous with 24 people. Nothing would make me happier than to be on podcasts, webinars, and conference stages, sharing with people who want to learn how to incorporate these ideas and principles into their lives. And I want to spend time with an entire community of people who are already famous with 12 people. Their stories and experiences fascinate me, and every conversation provides a chance to learn a nuance or twist on sharing wisdom in a way that benefits others.

There are so many quotes about immortality and eternity. I could combine the wisdom of the ancients and Russell Crowe by rounding out this book with, "What we do today will echo in eternity!" I could quote any number of the stoic philosophers or even Bruce Lee, "The key to immortality is living a life worth remembering." But I like what Mel Brooks has to say about the subject best.

"Immortality is a by-product of good work."

When I am gone, hopefully, many decades from now, I hope my work and the lives I have touched will mean that my name is still bouncing around in the atmosphere for a long time. It isn't that you or I should chase something as unrealistic as immortality, but we should strive to be a positive force and contributor of value to the people around us.

This is the reason for being famous with 12 people. You can fulfill this calling: being the person who made a difference in someone else's life. I am humbled when anyone stops me at a conference or in an airport hallway and says, "What you shared at that dinner last night got me thinking about how I can approach the challenge I'm facing differently."   I'm equally humbled when I hear, "What you said on stage meant a lot to me; I felt like someone finally understood the problem I'm trying to fix." These confirmations are always a surprise. They also fuel the passion that drives me to keep saying the quiet parts out loud and represent the unheard voices in my profession.

I hope that long after I'm gone, someone tells their child or friend, "This one time I heard Richard Bird say..."

While immortality is not our end goal, I also want that moment for you—that what you say, share, and learn on this journey echoes in eternity and that your good work lasts long after your expiration date arrives.

Thank you for reading this book. Thanks to the hundreds and maybe even thousands of friends, colleagues, and family who not only supported me through the process of writing this book but also were my greatest cheerleaders in sharing and promoting it. Thanks to my community and the universe of people in cybersecurity around the world who have given me a career, a passion, and an audience.

Life is a team sport. All the people I have thanked are part of my team, and I am on your team. If I can be a help, a resource, or a connector, I encourage you to reach out.

Go forth and conquer. You've got some getting famous to do.

www.ingramcontent.com/pod-product-compliance
Lightning Source LLC
Chambersburg PA
CBHW020230130626
46549CB00005B/1812